Table of Contents

The Wagner Family Tree . . . Page 5

Farm Life . . . Page 6

Appetizers, Snacks & Beverages . . . Page 8

Salads, Soups & Side Dishes . . . Page 36

Breads & Brunch . . . Page 66

Main Dishes . . . Page 82

Desserts . . . Page 110

Contributors:

Thanks to the following for swapping recipes and stories:

- Maxine Wagner, Jeri Cooper-Claire, Mary Cooper-Nichols, Judy Wagner,
- Tom Nichols, Greg Wagner, Arlene Quick, Rosemary Cooper, Sue Siler,
- Lynn Schumacher, Susan Thompson, Mildred Shinsky, Dolores Taylor,
- Karen Rambo, Pat Case, Pete Siler, Pat Lathrop, Mitz Lathrop, Eugene Lathrop, Dorothy Laufer, Betty Eames, Kathy Wagner, Bob Eames,
- Doris Hartman, Kelly Green, Lisa Ziemke, Vera VanDyke, June Strahan,
- Cheryl Blanchard, David Driscoll, Meagan Draper, Tracy Wagner,
- Jeff Wagner, Ed Wagner, Deanna Dorff, Ruth Ann Dittmer, Barb Greene,
- Sara Petersen-Walnus, Jeanine Petersen, Helen Cooper, Pat Keyser,
- Rita Johnson, Helen Wilson, Deb Lathrop, Michelle Soneral, Marjorie Sellner, Eileen Lemire, Mary Lue Dowell, Emma Wagner, Theresa Cooper,
- Henrietta Lemire, Jane Streeter, Helen Siler, Jean Bowles, Mary Jane Millard, Kate Murphy, Barb Dawson, Lauri Rambo and Bess Brye.

Book Design: Greg Wagner, Wagner Design, Inc.

Copywriting: Mike Dykstra

Copyright ©2020
fb.com/tailwaggindesign
gregwagner123@icloud.com

This cookbook is a collection of favorite recipes, which are not necessarily original recipes. All contributors are from Michigan unless otherwise noted. All rights reserved. No part of this publication may be reproduced in any form or by any means, electronic or mechanical, including photocopy and information storage and retrieval systems, without permission from the publisher.

Consumer advisory: Consuming raw or undercooked meats, poultry, seafood, shellfish or eggs may increase your risk of foodborne illness.

Enjoy! Greg Wagner

The Wagner Family Tree

My great grandfather, Frank Charles Rothweiler, journeyed from Baden, Germany to Indiana in 1867, when he was 27 years old. Over the course of the next seven years, he and his wife Josephine made their way to Ludington and purchased an 80-acre plot of land. "Rothweiler" had been Americanized to "Wagner" when Frank arrived on our shores, and this became the Wagner homestead.

Nobody really knows what Frank did in the old country, but he quickly set about building a home and planting crops in Ludington, enabling his family – which came to include children Adilia, Catherine, Louisa, George, Clara and Ida – to live comfortable, well-fed lives. (I'm choosing to believe they were happier than the picture below would indicate.)

George Wagner went on to marry Emma Albrecht and inherit the farm. They had five children: Veronica, Mildred, Helen, Maxine and George II. That's Emma (seated) and her kids in the middle photo.

When George I died, Uncle Bud and Aunt Ve ran the farm until George II (my dad) was old enough to take over. Dad married Maxine Anne Lemire (right photo) in 1947, and they had nine children: George III, Edmund, Susan, Bruce, Gregory (that's me!), John, Jeffrey, Wayne and Marc.

Attendance at today's Wagner Family Reunions continues to mount, as aunts and uncles and cousins and grandchildren and great grandchildren mingle with neighbors and friends who fondly recall the heyday of George and Maxine. My parents have passed away, but their legacy lives on in the memories we all hold dear.

Farm Life

Ludington sits smack dab in the middle of Michigan's Fruit Belt, a narrow swath across the western side of the state blessed with fertile soil, rolling topography and the tempering climate of Lake Michigan.

These conditions are ideal for growing all sorts of fruit, and the Wagners cultivated apples, cherries, peaches, pears, plums, apricots, crabapples and strawberries for commercial sale. We kept some of the harvest for ourselves, of course, and we also maintained a massive vegetable garden.

Dad was an inventive sort of man who modernized the farm with new plantings and new technologies – like the cherry picker he built from scratch. His handyman skills, honed under the direction of Grandpa Lemire, were a tremendous asset in a household of nine rambunctious kids. (Anything that could get broken, did.)

Mom grew up a city girl, but she knew her way around a kitchen. In addition to cooking and baking, she canned and froze more than 1,000 quarts of fruits and vegetables each year.

Mom and dad taught us to work hard by example (though I don't recall much choice in the matter). They also taught us how to entertain. Sunday dinners were huge social events, and there was always room for relatives and friends. Half the county was invited to our legendary corn roasts, and a good time was had by all.

That spirit of hospitality was passed down to my siblings and me. I love to cook. I love to use farm-fresh ingredients. And I love to treat guests to a taste of Wagner family tradition.

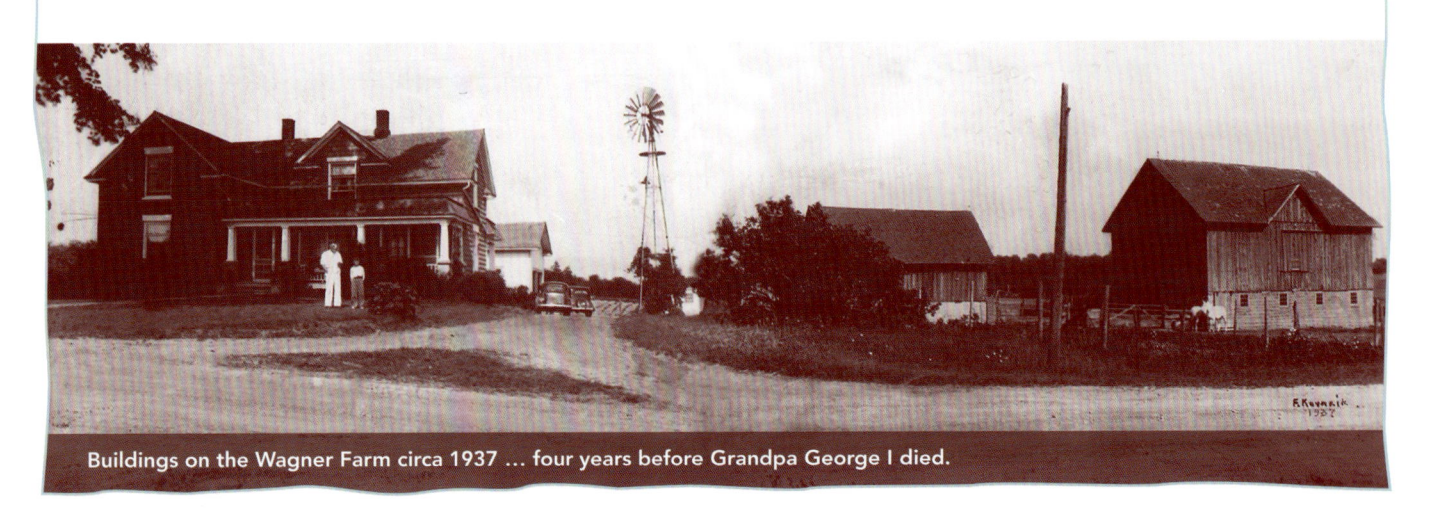

Buildings on the Wagner Farm circa 1937 … four years before Grandpa George I died.

Stylin' in the apple orchard: Grandma Lemire, Mom and "kissin' cousin" Harriet Purucker, sporting her signature gravity-defying 'do.

My brother George outside the General Store owned by Aunt Helen and Uncle LaVern. It was a frequent party site.

My dad stands between Uncle Bud and Aunt Helen on the Wagner farm. Can you spot Uncle Frank in a tree?

My dad and his trenchcoat-wearing, fedora-sporting cousin Ron. (Not an approved farm uniform.)

Millions of apples and cherries were delivered to processors on our "company truck" through the years.

Mom in the Lemire family garden, 'round about 1944.

7

No-Bake Spicy Caramel Corn, page 29

APPETIZERS, SNACKS & BEVERAGES

Party Meatballs

Maxine Wagner, Ludington

3 lb. ground beef or turkey
2 small onions, diced
2 green peppers, diced
3 cloves of garlic, minced
2-1/4 tsp. salt
1-1/2 cups bread crumbs
1 bottle (18 oz.) barbecue sauce

Preheat oven to 325°. In large bowl, combine meat, onions, peppers, garlic, salt and bread crumbs until thoroughly mixed. Roll into 1" balls. Place close together in a 13" x 9" cake pan. Cover with warm water. Bake for 1 hour. Drain meatballs. Cover with barbecue sauce and heat before serving. Works well in a slow cooker. Yield: 100 meatballs.

Party Cheese Ball

Jeri Cooper-Claire, Ludington

2 bricks (8 oz.) cream cheese
2 T. onions, chopped
1/4 cup green peppers, chopped
1 can (8 oz.) crushed pineapple, well drained
1 cup pecans, finely chopped

Combine all ingredients except pecans in a bowl. Mix well. Shape into one ball. Roll in pecans. Wrap in plastic wrap and refrigerate overnight. Yield: 1 cheese ball.

On a family trip, Mom charmed the chef at a popular Wisconsin Dells restaurant to snag this meatball recipe. It became a staple of her parties.

There are people who like their veggies to go down smooth and people who like 'em with a little kick. Choose wisely. Or serve both!

Vegetable Dip

Mary Cooper-Nichols, Ludington

1 cup mayonnaise
1 cup sour cream
1 T. onions, minced
1/4 tsp. dried parsley
1/2 tsp. dill weed
1/4 tsp. salt
1/2 tsp. seasoned salt
1/2 tsp. ground pepper

- Combine all ingredients until blended. Chill and serve. Yield: 32 servings.

Zippy Vegetable Dip

Maxine Wagner, Ludington

1 cup mayonnaise
1 T. onions, minced
1 T. horseradish
1 T. white vinegar
1/4 tsp. curry powder

- Combine all ingredients until blended. Chill and serve. Yield: 16 servings.

Crab Meat Dip

Jeri Cooper-Claire, Ludington

1 brick (8 oz.) cream cheese, softened
2 T. Worcestershire sauce
1 T. lemon juice
2 T. mayonnaise
1/2 cup onions, chopped
Dash of salt
1 can (4.25 oz.) flaked crab meat, well drained
3/4 cup chili sauce

Mix creamed cheese, Worcestershire sauce, lemon juice, mayonnaise, onions and salt until smooth. In a small bowl, combine crab meat and chili sauce. Pour over cheese mixture just before serving. Yield: 30 servings.

Spinach Dip

Maxine Wagner, Ludington

1 pkg. (10 oz.) frozen spinach, thawed
1 cup mayonnaise
1/2 cup sour cream
3 T. grated parmesan cheese
1 T. dried onion flakes
1/2 tsp. seasoned salt
1/4 tsp. ground pepper
1/4 tsp. garlic powder
1/4 cup water chestnuts, sliced and quartered

Press water out of thawed spinach and chop. In a mixing bowl, combine all ingredients. Chill and serve. Yield: 18 servings.

I never encountered any crabs in Lake Michigan, but that didn't stop cousin Jeri from developing this perfect party appetizer.

There are no oysters in Lake Michigan, either. Nor are there any in this recipe. It's fake news, people!

Ranch Oyster Crackers

Maxine Wagner, Ludington

- 1 pkg. (16 oz.) plain oyster crackers
- 1 pkg. ranch buttermilk salad dressing mix
- 1/4 cup vegetable oil
- 1/4 tsp. lemon pepper
- 1/2 tsp. dill weed
- 1/4 tsp. garlic powder

- Preheat oven to 325°. Combine ranch mix and oil in small bowl. Add lemon pepper, dill weed and garlic powder. In a large bowl, place oyster crackers and pour ranch mix over the crackers, and stir until well coated. Spread crackers out on a jelly roll pan. Bake for 15-20 minutes. Yield: 8 cups.

Easy Chili Dip

Maxine Wagner, Ludington

- 1 cup chili sauce
- 1/2 cup mayonnaise
- 1 T. horseradish
- 1/4 cup cottage cheese

- Combine all ingredients until blended. Chill and serve. Yield: 20 servings.

Beef & Cream Cheese Spread

Judy Wagner, Ludington

- 1 brick (8 oz.) cream cheese, softened
- 2 T. milk
- 1 pkg. (3 oz.) dried beef, chopped
- 1/2 cup green pepper, diced
- 1 T. onion flakes
- 2 T. butter
- 1/2 tsp. garlic, minced
- 1/2 cup sour cream

Blend cheese with milk in medium-sized bowl. Add beef, green pepper, onion flakes, butter and garlic. Fold in sour cream. Bake at 350° for 20 minutes. Yield: 8 servings.

Marinated Mushrooms

Maxine Wagner, Ludington

- 4 cans (4 oz.) whole mushrooms
- 1-1/3 cups garlic vinaigrette dressing
- 1/2 cup green peppers, sliced thin
- 1 jar (4 oz.) diced pimentos
- 1 medium onion, sliced thin

Drain mushrooms. In medium bowl, combine all ingredients. Refrigerate and let stand overnight to marinate. Yield: 8 servings.

We didn't grow mushrooms as a crop, but we knew the nooks and crannies where they popped up around the farm – and Mom loved to cook with them.

A nod to our German heritage, these sausage-and-sauerkraut bites were all the rage at family gatherings. Even kids love 'em. (Well, kids with good taste.)

Easy Chili Dip

Tom Nichols, Ludington

1 brick (8 oz.) cream cheese
2 slices of garlic dill pickles (favorite brand)
2 T. juice from the pickle jar

- Put all ingredients into a blender/chopper and puree until desired texture. A few splashes of milk to the mixture may be added to reach desired thickness. Stores well in refrigerator for up to 5 days. Yield: 1-1/2 cups.

Sauerkraut Balls

Maxine Wagner, Ludington

2-1/2 cups sauerkraut, drained and chopped
1 lb. bulk sausage
1 lb. ground beef or turkey
1/2 cup onions, diced
3 T. dried parsley
1 tsp. garlic powder
1/2 tsp. dry mustard
1 tsp. salt
1/8 tsp. pepper
1 T. sugar
2 eggs, well beaten
1/4 cup milk
1/2 cup bread crumbs

- In a large bowl, mix sauerkraut, sausage, beef or turkey, onions, parsley, garlic powder, dry mustard, salt, pepper and sugar. In a separate bowl, mix eggs and milk. Roll into 1" balls. Dip balls in the milk/egg mixture and roll in the bread crumbs. Place on a greased jelly roll pan. Place in oven under the broiler for 1-2 minutes or until done. Yield: approximately 6 dozen sauerkraut balls.

Spinach Balls

Greg Wagner, Caledonia

2 pkgs. (9 oz.) spinach
1 pkg. (14 oz.) seasoned stuffing mix
2 small onions, diced fine
6 eggs, beaten
1 T. garlic salt
1/2 tsp. pepper
3/4 cup melted butter
1/2 cup grated parmesan cheese

- Thaw and press the water out of the spinach and coarsely chop. In a large bowl, combine spinach, stuffing mix, onions, eggs, garlic salt, pepper, butter and parmesan cheese. Mix well. Roll into 1" balls and place on a greased cookie sheet. Bake at 350° for 20 minutes. Yield: 2 dozen spinach balls.

> As far as I'm concerned, anything with "veggie" in the title is a health food (cream cheese and sour cream notwithstanding).

Veggie Pizza

Arlene Quick, Ludington

- 2 cans (8 oz.) refrigerated crescent rolls or sheets
- 2 bricks (8 oz.) cream cheese, softened
- 1 pkg. ranch buttermilk salad dressing mix
- 1 cup sour cream
- 1 tsp. dill weed
- Various vegetables cut in small pieces (broccoli, cauliflower, onions, peppers, carrots, olives, etc.)

Preheat oven to 375°. Spread crescent roll dough onto a cookie sheet. Bake dough about 10 minutes or until done. Mix cream cheese, dressing mix, sour cream and dill weed together until blended. Spread evenly over the cooked dough. Top with cut vegetables of your choice. Yield: 20 servings.

Jezebel Sauce

Greg Wagner, Caledonia

- 1/2 cup pineapple topping
- 1/2 cup apple jelly
- 2 tsp. horseradish
- 1 tsp. dry mustard
- 1/2 tsp. coarse black pepper
- 1 brick (8 oz.) cream cheese

Combine pineapple topping, apple jelly, horseradish, dry mustard and pepper until blended. Serve over a brick of cream cheese with crackers. Yield: 20 servings.

Dilly Beans stay crunchy and flavorful long after canning. I've heard tell some people use them as a Bloody Mary garnish, but I'm not naming names.

Shrimp Cocktail Sauce

Maxine Wagner, Ludington

1/2 cup chili sauce
1/3 cup ketchup
2 T. horseradish
1-1/2 tsp. Worcestershire sauce
2 T. lemon juice
2-3 drops tabasco sauce

Mix all ingredients together and chill. Serve with chilled, cooked shrimp. Yield: 8 servings.

Tartar Sauce

Greg Wagner, Caledonia

1 cup mayonnaise
1/4 cup dill pickle, chopped
1/4 tsp. Worcestershire sauce
1 T. lemon juice
1 T. onion, minced

Mix all ingredients together and chill. Yield: 8 servings.

Dilly Beans

Rosemary Cooper, Freeport

2 lbs. string beans, trimmed
1 tsp. cayenne pepper*
4 cloves garlic
4 heads fresh dill
2-1/2 cups cider vinegar
2-1/2 cups water
1/4 cup salt

*Option: substitute 1 T. horseradish in place of cayenne pepper per jar

Pack beans lengthwise into hot pint jars. To each pint add 1/4 tsp. cayenne pepper, 1 clove garlic and 1 head of dill. In a large saucepan, combine vinegar, water and salt. Bring to boil. Pour hot mixture over the beans leaving 1/2" headspace. Remove air bubbles by inserting a handle of a spoon into the jar. Process pint jars for 10 minutes in a boiling water bath. Yield: 4 pints.

Pickled Onions

Mary Cooper-Nichols, Ludington

- 1 cup apple cider vinegar
- 2/3 cup white sugar
- 1 T. picking salt
- 1 tsp. mustard seed
- 1 tsp. pickling spice
- 1/4 tsp. thyme
- 2 large red onions, sliced in thin rings
- 2 large white onions, sliced in thin rings

In a large pan, bring the first 6 ingredients to a boil. Add onions to boiling mixture, reduce heat and simmer 5 minutes. Place onion mixture in pint canning jars and process in a hot water bath for 10 minutes or place in airtight container and place in refrigerator. Onions will keep for up to 2 months in the vinegar brine. Yield: 5 pints.

Pickled Beets

Maxine Wagner, Ludington

- 6 lbs. of 2" to 2-1/2" diameter beets
- 15-18 whole cloves
- 3 cups white vinegar
- 1-1/2 cups water
- 2-1/2 cups sugar
- 2 tsp. salt

Trim off beet tops, leaving 1" of stem. Wash thoroughly. In a large pan, boil beets for 25-30 minutes or until tender. Cool beets. Trim off roots and stems and slip off skins. Slice into 1/4" slices or in quarters. Place 3 whole cloves in the bottom of each sterilized pint jar. In a separate pan, combine vinegar, water, sugar and salt, and bring to boil. Place beets in canning jars. Pour hot liquid over the beets leaving 1/2" headspace. Process in a hot water bath for 10 minutes. Yield: 5-6 pints.

Pickled pink: I love the vibrant color of these pickled veggies. They'll look great on your pantry shelf.

Bread & Butter Pickles were the bread & butter of my Mom's pantry – a fresh taste of the garden to enjoy all winter.

Bread & Butter Pickles

Maxine Wagner, Ludington

4 qts. sliced pickles
6 medium onions, sliced
1 green pepper, sliced in narrow strips
1 red pepper, sliced in narrow strips
3 gloves of garlic
1/3 cup salt
Ice cubes
5 cups sugar
3 cups white vinegar
1-1/2 tsp. turmeric
1-1/2 tsp. celery seed
2 T. mustard seed

In a large canning kettle, layer pickles, onions, peppers and garlic cloves. Sprinkle the salt over the layers. Mix a few cups of ice into the layers. Then top with ice. Let stand 3 hours. Drain thoroughly. Divide pickle mixture into two batches and cook in two kettles. In separate bowl, combine sugar, vinegar and spices. Pour equally over the two kettles of pickle mixture. Heat to just boiling. Place hot mixture in pint canning jars and process in a hot water bath for 15 minutes. Yield: 6-7 pints.

Sue's Salsa

Sue Siler, Alto

4 cups romano tomatoes, peeled and chopped
3 cups green pepper, chopped
1 cup onion, chopped
2 cloves garlic, chopped fine
2 jalepeno peppers, chopped with seeds
1 cup white vinegar
1-1/2 T. salt
3 T. sugar
1 can (12 oz.) tomato paste
1 can (15 oz.) black beans, rinsed and drained
1 cup frozen corn, thawed

In a large pot, mix all ingredients. Bring to boil and cook over low heat for 20 minutes. Add tomato paste, beans and corn. Bring mixture back to boil. Ladle hot mixture into sterilized pint canning jars and process in a hot water bath for 20 minutes. Yield: 5 pints.

I know people get intimidated by the idea of canning ... but it's really not as difficult as it seems. And the taste is well worth it!

Cucumber Relish

Sue Siler, Alto

4-1/2 quarts cucumber, ground
4 cups onions, ground
4 cups celery, ground
2 jalepeno peppers, ground
2 quarts water
1/2 cup salt
4 cups white vinegar
2 cups water
4 cups sugar
1 tsp. turmeric
1 T. celery seed
1 T. mustard seed

In large pan, soak cucumber, onions, celery, peppers, water and salt, and store in refrigerator overnight. Thoroughly drain vegetable mixture. In large canning kettle, bring vinegar, water, sugar, turmeric, celery seed and mustard seed to a boil and simmer for 10 minutes. Add the cucumber mixture to the boiling liquid and simmer for 10 more minutes. Ladle hot mixture into sterilized pint canning jars and process in a hot water bath for 10 minutes. Yield: 12 pints.

Trust me, there's only so much zucchini bread your family can take. Here's another tasty way to utilize this summer squash.

Zucchini Relish

Lynn Schumacher, Caledonia

10 cups zucchini, chopped
4 cups onions, chopped
4 cups red peppers, chopped
1/3 cup salt
1-3/4 cups white vinegar
3/4 cup apple juice or cider
4-1/2 cups sugar
2 T. cornstarch
1 tsp. turmeric
1 tsp. celery seed
1 tsp. nutmeg
1/2 tsp. pepper

In large pan, soak zucchini, onions, peppers and salt in water, and store in refrigerator overnight. The next day, strain and rinse the vegetables with cold water and drain. In large canning kettle, bring vinegar, juice, sugar, cornstarch, turmeric, celery seed, nutmeg and pepper to a boil. Then add vegetables and simmer for 20 minutes. Ladle hot mixture into sterilized pint canning jars and process in a hot water bath for 10 minutes. Yield: 7-9 pints.

Sue's Chili Sauce

Sue Siler, Alto

24 large tomatoes, scalded, peeled and chopped
4 large onions, chopped
3 green peppers, chopped
2 T. salt
1 T. cinnamon
1/2 tsp. allspice
2-1/2 cups sugar
2 cups white vinegar

In a large pot, mix all ingredients. Bring to a boil and cook over low heat for at least 4 hours, stirring frequently so it does not stick and burn. Ladle hot mixture into sterilized pint canning jars and process in a hot water bath for 10 minutes. This is delicious on beef roast and meatloaf. Yield: 6-7 pints.

Fruit Pizza

Susan Thompson, Scottville

1 roll of sugar cookie dough
1 brick (8 oz.) cream cheese, softened
1/2 cup sugar
1 tsp. vanilla extract
Fresh fruit of your choice: strawberries, blueberries, kiwi, bananas, grapes, pineapple, etc.

Glaze
3/4 cup water
1 cup orange juice
1/4 cup lemon juice
1/4 tsp. salt
3 T. cornstarch
1 cup sugar

Preheat oven to 350°. Spread cookie dough onto a greased pizza or jelly roll pan. Bake dough about 14-18 minutes or until golden brown. Let cool. In a small bowl, mix cream cheese, sugar and vanilla together until blended. Spread evenly oven the baked dough. Top with fruit of your choice.

For the glaze: Place all ingredients in saucepan. Boil one minute. Cool slightly. Drizzle glaze over the top of the fruit. Refrigerate. Yield: 12 servings.

This dessert pizza looks as good as it tastes — and it's chock-full of healthy antioxidants. And cream cheese. (The Lord giveth and the Lord taketh away.)

You don't have to go to Michigan's Mackinac Island for great fudge – it's easy to make your own smooth, creamy, delectable fudge at home.

Graham Cracker Fudge

Mildred Shinsky, Flint

- 2 oz. baker's unsweetened chocolate
- 1 can (14 oz.) sweetened condensed milk
- 1 /2 tsp. vanilla extract
- 1-1/2 cups graham cracker crumbs
- 1 cup walnuts or pecans, chopped
- 1 T. butter

In a large saucepan, cook all ingredients until thickened. Pour into a buttered 9" x 9" pan. Cool. Cut into squares. Yield: 16 pieces.

White Chocolate Cherry Fudge

Greg Wagner, Caledonia

- 2-1/2 cups confectioner's sugar
- 3/4 cup half-and-half cream
- 1/4 cup (1/2 stick) butter
- 1 pkg. (12 oz.) white chocolate chips
- 1-1/4 cup dried tart cherries, chopped
- 1/2 tsp. vanilla extract

In saucepan over medium heat, combine confectioner's sugar and half-and-half. Add butter and bring to a boil, stirring constantly. Once mixture reaches a boil, stop stirring and let it cook for 5 minutes. It will be thick. Reduce heat to low and add white chocolate chips, stirring until smooth. Stir in cherries and vanilla. Pour into a well-buttered 9" x 9" pan. Chill. Cut in squares. Yield: 20 pieces.

9-Minute Fudge

Dolores Taylor, Ludington

- 1-1/3 cups butter
- 4-1/2 cups sugar
- 1 can (12 oz.) evaporated milk
- 1 jar (8 oz.) marshmallow creme
- 3 pkgs. (12 oz.) semi-sweet chocolate chips
- 2 tsp. vanilla extract
- 2 cups pecans or walnuts, chopped

In saucepan, melt butter, sugar and evaporated milk. Bring to boil, stirring constantly for 9 minutes. Remove from heat and add marshmallow creme and chocolate chips. Stir until well blended. Stir in vanilla and nuts and pour into a buttered 13" x 9" pan. Chill. Yield: 96 pieces.

Double Chocolate Fudge

Karen Rambo, Washington Courthouse, Ohio

- 1 can (14 oz.) sweetened condensed milk
- 2 cups (12 oz. pkg.) semi-sweet chocolate chips
- 1 oz. unsweetened baking chocolate
- 1 tsp. vanilla extract
- 1-1/2 cups pecans or walnuts, chopped

In microwavable bowl, combine milk, chocolate chips and baking chocolate. Microwave on high for 1 minute. Stir. Heat for about an additional 2 minutes. Stir until smooth. Stir in vanilla and nuts and spread evenly into a buttered 9" x 9" pan. Chill. Yield: 36 pieces.

Ohhhhh fudge! A not-so-fast recipe ... but delicious. OR a really fast and easy recipe ... equally delicious.

You might also know these as Buckeye Balls – but we don't use the "B" word in Michigan. (That's "B" as in Buckeyes, the accursed Ohio State football team.)

Peanut Butter Bon Bons

Pat Case, Petoskey

- 2 cups smooth peanut butter
- 1/2 cup (1 stick) butter or margarine
- 4-1/2 cups confectioner's sugar
- 3 cups crisp rice cereal
- 2 cups semi-sweet chocolate chips

In saucepan, melt peanut butter and butter. In large bowl, combine confectioner's sugar and cereal. Pour warm peanut butter mixture over cereal. Blend together with buttered hands. Form in 1/2" balls and place on a cookie sheet. Chill until firm. Melt chocolate in double boiler. Either dip half of the peanut butter ball in the chocolate or immerse the whole ball and place on a waxed paper-lined cookie sheet. Chill. Yield: 80-90 bon bons.

Dad's sister Mildred and Mom's sister Pat bought the sweets. Good cooks run on both sides of the family!

Peanut Candy Squares

Mildred Shinsky, Flint

6 cups rice cereal squares
1 cup peanuts
1 cup sugar
1 cup light corn syrup
1 cup smooth peanut butter
1 tsp. vanilla extract

In a large bowl, mix cereal and peanuts. Line a 13" x 9" pan with foil. Bring sugar, corn syrup and peanut butter to a boil over medium heat. Boil for one minute. Add vanilla and stir well. Pour over cereal and nuts. Stir to coat. Pour into foil lined pan. Cool. Break or cut into pieces. Yield: 20 pieces.

Mocha Balls

Pat Case, Petoskey

1 cup butter, softened
1/2 cup sugar
1 tsp. vanilla extract
2 cups all-purpose flour
1/4 cup cocoa
1 tsp. instant coffee granules
1/4 tsp. salt
1 cup walnuts, chopped
1/2 cup maraschino cherries, chopped
Confectioner's sugar

In mixing bowl, cream butter, sugar and vanilla until light and fluffy. In a separate bowl, stir flour, cocoa, coffee granules and salt. Gradually beat into creamed mixture. Stir in walnuts and cherries. Chill 1 hour. Shape into 1" balls. Place on cookie sheet and bake at 325° for 20 minutes. Cool on rack and dust with confectioner's sugar. Yield: 20-30 balls.

You don't need to be a chocolatier to make these magically sweet treats at home. Get ready to impress your friends!

Sea Foam

Greg Wagner, Caledonia

- 1 cup dark corn syrup
- 1 cup sugar
- 1 T. white vinegar
- 1 T. baking soda
- 2 oz. baker's unsweetened chocolate
- 1 pkg. (16 oz.) chocolate candy coating
- 1/2 cup semi-sweet chocolate chips

Butter the surface of a 13" x 9" jelly roll pan. In large saucepan, stir corn syrup, sugar and vinegar, and bring to a boil over high heat. Boil until mixture reaches 300°. Take off heat. Quickly stir in the baking soda. Only stir until mixed then pour onto the buttered pan. Do NOT spread the mixture. Let it spread on its own. This will make a fluffier foam. Let cool. Break the foam up into small pieces with a sharp knife.

In double boiler, melt baker's chocolate, candy coating and chocolate chips until smooth. Dip the foam pieces with a teaspoon into the melted chocolate and place on foil. If chocolate gets thick, thin it with a dab of shortening. Let cool. Yield: 80-100 pieces.

Pete's Peanut Brittle

Pete Siler, Alto

I don't want to cast stones at anyone else's peanut brittle, but this is hands-down the best I have ever tasted. (And I've tasted a lot.)

1-1/2 tsp. baking soda
1 tsp. water
1 tsp. vanilla extract
1-1/2 cups sugar
1 cup water
1 cup light corn syrup
3 T. butter
1 lb. raw (unroasted) peanuts, shelled

Preheat oven to 200°. Spray 2 cookie sheets with cooking spray and place in the warm oven. Also spray a large spatula with oil and set aside. In a small dish, combine baking soda, water and vanilla. In an 8 qt. pot, combine sugar, water and corn syrup, and cook over medium heat until the mixture reaches 245°. Stir in the butter and peanuts. When the mixture reaches 250°, remove cookie sheets from oven and place on wire racks. Cook mixture, stirring constantly until it reaches 305°. Remove from heat and add the soda mixture. Stir vigorously and move quickly to pour on the cookie sheets, dividing it as evenly as possible with the coated spatula. Spread the brittle as THIN as possible. Let cool (about 15-20 minutes). Carefully remove the brittle from the cookie sheets and place on paper towels to absorb the cooking spray. Break into pieces and store in an airtight container. Yield: 4 (8 oz.) servings.

Think of these two caramel corn recipes as Original and Extra Zippy. Personally, I love the combo of sweet and spicy.

Caramel Corn

Pat Lathrop, Ludington

- 20-24 cups popped popcorn
- 1 cup (2 sticks) butter
- 2 cups brown sugar
- 1 cup light corn syrup
- 1 tsp. vanilla extract
- 1 tsp. baking soda
- 1 tsp. salt (opt.)

In saucepan, melt butter, sugar and corn syrup. Boil 5 minutes. Add vanilla, baking soda and salt (opt.). Stir until blended. Pour over popcorn and stir gently until coated. Place in baking pans and bake at 250° for 45 minutes, stirring every 15 minutes. Let cool and store in airtight container. Yield: 40 servings.

No-Bake Spicy Caramel Corn

Greg Wagner, Caledonia

- 1/3 cup butter
- 2/3 cup brown sugar
- 1/4 tsp. cayenne pepper
- 1 tsp. cinnamon
- 6 cups popcorn
- 3 cups small pretzels
- 1-1/2 cups toasted pecan halves

In a large bowl, combine popcorn, pretzels and pecans and set aside. In a saucepan, melt butter and sugar. Stir in cayenne pepper and cinnamon. Bring to boil and cook for 2 minutes. Pour over popcorn mixture and stir gently until coated. Let cool and store in an airtight container. Yield: 20 servings.

Chocolate-Filled Bon Bons
Maxine Wagner, Ludington

3/4 cup shortening
1/2 cup sugar
1/4 cup brown sugar
1 egg
2 tsp. vanilla extract
1/2 tsp. almond extract
1-3/4 cup all-purpose flour
1/2 tsp. baking powder
1/2 tsp. salt
1/2 cup almond, chopped
42-48 chocolate kisses

- In mixing bowl, cream shortening and sugars together. Add egg, vanilla and almond extracts. Blend in flour, baking powder, salt and almonds. Form into 1" balls. Press each ball around a kiss so kiss is completely covered. Bake at 350° on a cookie sheet for 12 minutes. Yield: 42-48 bon bons.

Caramel Delights
Pat Case, Petoskey

1/2 lb. caramels (28 squares)
2 T. heavy cream
1-1/4 cups pecan halves
1/2-1 cup semi-sweet chocolate chips

Melt caramels in a double boiler. Stir in cream until smooth. Add pecans. Drop by teaspoonfuls onto a well-greased baking sheet. Refrigerate. In double boiler, melt semi-sweet chocolate chips. Remove from heat. Dip caramels in chocolate, place back on baking sheet and refrigerate.
Yield: 30 pieces.

Remember the good old days, when housewives would sit around and eat bon bons all day? Yeah, neither do I — they were too busy cooking!

You will never be satisfied with the store-bought version once you try this recipe. I get the whole family involved in assembling them.

Chocolate-Covered Cherries

Greg Wagner, Caledonia

- 4 cups confectioner's sugar
- 4 T. butter or margarine, softened
- 1/4 cup cherry juice
- 1-2 jars (10 oz.) maraschino cherries, juice reserved
- 2 oz. baker's unsweetened chocolate
- 1 pkg. (16 oz. block) chocolate candy coating
- 1/2 cup semi-sweet chocolate chips
- 1/2 cup red candy melts for drizzle decoration (optional)

Drain cherries, reserving the juice. Lay cherries on paper towels and pat them until they are as dry as possible. In a medium size bowl, mix sugar, butter and cherry juice until mixture forms a soft dough. Wrap in plastic wrap and chill for 20 minutes. Flatten a small amount of dough in the palm of your hand (slightly dust the palm of your hand with confectioner's sugar so dough doesn't stick). Place a dry cherry in the center of the dough and wrap the cherry with the dough. Roll in your hands to completely cover the cherry. Place on a wax paper-lined jelly roll pan. Refrigerate for 20 minutes. Melt all the chocolate in a double boiler. Dip the dough-covered cherry into the chocolate with a small spoon. Carefully place on a foil-covered baking sheet. Chill. For decoration, melt colored candy coating wafers. If the candy is too thick, add a bit of shortening to the melted coating until it is thin enough to drizzle. Refrigerate up to 4 weeks. Yield: 40-50 cherries.

Eggnog

Mitz Lathrop, Ludington

Custard
1/2 cup sugar
3 egg yolks
1/4 tsp. salt
4 cups whole milk, scalded

Whipped Egg Whites
1/8 tsp. salt
3 egg whites
1/4 cup sugar
1/2 tsp. vanilla extract

In mixing bowl, beat sugar and egg yolks. Add salt and slowly stir in milk. Cook in a double boiler until mixture coats a metal spoon. Cool. In separate bowl add salt and egg whites. Beat until stiff. Add sugar and vanilla and beat well. Fold egg whites into the custard. Mix throughly and chill at least 4 hours. Pile into punch cups. Sprinkle with nutmeg and add a cinnamon stir stick. Dark rum can also be stirred into the cup if desired. Yield: 6-8 cups.

Fruit Punch

Maxine Wagner, Ludington

1 can (12 oz.) frozen orange juice
1 can (12 oz.) frozen lemonade
2 cans (40 oz.) unsweetened pineapple juice
1/4 cup lime juice
8 cups cold water
2-1/2 cups sugar
2 liters ginger ale
1 liter club soda

Mix all ingredients in large container. Pour into punch bowl. Add ice, sliced strawberries and oranges. Yield: 46 cups.

Coffee Liqueur

Eugene Lathrop, Ludington

3 cups white sugar
12 tsp. (rounded) instant coffee
4 cups water
1/5 bottle of vodka
3 tsp. vanilla extract

In large saucepan, combine sugar, coffee granules and water. Bring to boil and simmer for one hour. Remove from heat and cool. Add vodka and vanilla. Pour in bottles. Yield: 6 (12.5 oz.) bottles.

This is the eggnog my Aunt Mitz made for people who hate eggnog. If they still didn't like it, she added rum. Lots of rum.

I won't tell your party guests how easy it was to make these liqueurs if you won't. They make great gifts, too!

Mocha Cream Liqueur
Maxine Wagner, Ludington

1 can (14 oz.) sweetened condensed milk
2 cups light cream or milk
1 T. instant coffee granules
1 egg yolk, beaten
1 cup Irish whiskey
1/2 cup coffee liqueur
3 T. chocolate syrup

In large saucepan, combine condensed milk, cream and coffee granules. Cook over medium heat until coffee granules are dissolved. Gradually add half the heated mixutre into the egg yolk and stir quickly. Pour egg yolk mixture into the milk mixture. Bring to boil. Cook over medium heat until thick and bubbly, stirring constantly. Remove from heat and stir in whiskey, coffee liqueur and syrup. Cool. Pour in bottles. Store in refrigerator for up to 2 months. Yield: 4-5 cups liqueur.

Orange Liqueur
Dorothy Laufer, Ludington

1 cup water
2 cups sugar
2 orange peelings
2 tsp. vanilla extract
3 T. orange extract
1 tsp. lemon extract
8 drops yellow food coloring
1 drop red food coloring
2 cups vodka

In large saucepan, combine water, sugar and orange peel. Boil for 5 minutes. Remove from heat and add extracts and food colorings. Let cool and strain with cheesecloth. Add vodka. Pour in bottles. Yield: 3-4 cups liqueur.

Margarita
Lime wedge garnish
Kosher salt, for the rim
1-1/2 oz. (3 T.) tequila
1 oz. orange liqueur
1-1/2 T. fresh lime juice

Cut a notch in a lime wedge, then run the lime around the rim of a glass. Dip the edge of the rim into a plate of salt. Place tequilla, liqueur and lime juice in a cocktail shaker with 4 ice cubes and shake until cold. Strain into the glass. Fill the glass with ice and serve. Yield: 1 drink.

Cherry Bounce

Betty Eames, Door County, Wisconsin

2 qts. fresh tart cherries
4 cups vodka or brandy
2 cups sugar
2 (1 qt.) canning jars and lids

- Place 1 qt. tart cherries in each jar. Pour one cup of sugar over cherries in each jar and 2 cups of vodka over the sugar-covered cherries. Cover tightly with lid. Turn over a few times to make sure sugar is dissolved completely. Store in a cool place for at least 8 weeks. Pour the liqueur out of the jars into cordial glasses and serve at room temperature. Or serve on vanilla ice cream! Yield: 2 quarts.

Grasshopper

Betty Eames, Door County, Wisconsin

2 cups vanilla ice cream
1 oz. green crème de menthe
1 oz. white crème de cacao
Whipped cream for garnish

- Blend the ice cream, 1/2 oz. crème de menthe and 1 oz. crème de cacao in a blender. Pour into a cocktail glass. Top with a dollop of whipped cream and drizzle the remaining crème de menthe over the top. Yield: 4 drinks.

Hot Buttered Rum

Kathy Wagner, Caledonia

1 lb. pkg. (2-1/3 cups) brown sugar
1/2 cup (1 stick) butter or margarine, softened
1/4 tsp. nutmeg
1/2 tsp. cinnamon
1/2 tsp. cloves
Dark rum

- In small bowl, cream sugar and butter. Add spices to make base mix. In a mug, pour 1.5 oz. rum and 1 heaping tablespoon of base mix. Fill cup with boiling water and stir. Base keeps in refrigerator for months. Yield: 24 servings.

Cherry Bounce comes from Wisconsin via my friend Betty's mother-in-law Esther. Store in a cool place until Thanksgiving so you'll have something to be extra thankful for.

Reminiscent of that famous store brand, this recipe is packed with vegetables – but it tastes so much fresher, enjoyed on its own or as a Bloody Mary base.

Pete's Tomato Juice
Pete Siler, Alto

1 peck (8 qts.) tomatoes
3 large onions
3 large green peppers
2 red chili peppers
4 stalks celery, including leaves
5 stems and leaves of fresh parsley
8 tsp. salt
8 tsp. sugar
2 tsp. pepper

Wash and core tomatoes and wash and cut the other ingredients. In a 5-cup blender, finely grind 4 cups of tomatoes. Pour into a large pot. Finely grind onions, peppers, celery and parsley until you have 5 cups. Pour this mixture into the pot with the tomato puree. Repeat the process until all ingredients are liquified. Next, heat the mixture to a boil (stirring occasionally to keep from sticking). Boil for 3-5 minutes, stirring occasionally. Run this mixture through a food mill to remove seeds and pour into a 10-12 quart stockpot. Once the juice is separated, heat to a boil, adding salt, sugar and pepper. Pour the hot juice into sterilized quart jars. Process in a hot water bath for 10 minutes. Makes an amazing Bloody Mary. Yield: 8 quarts.

Brandy Alexander
Bob Eames, Grand Rapids

1-1/2 oz. (1 shot) brandy
1-1/2 oz. (1 shot) crème de cacao
1-1/2 oz. (1 shot) half & half cream

Version 2
3 oz. brandy
3 oz. crème de cacao
1 scoop vanilla ice cream

Combine all 3 ingredients in a cocktail shaker. Add ice and shake until well chilled. Strain into a chilled coupe or martini glass. Garnish with grated or ground nutmeg. Yield: 1 serving.

Version 2: In a blender, combine all ingredients until smooth. Serve in chilled coupe or martini glasses. Garnish with grated or ground nutmeg. Yield: 2 servings.

Strawberry Daiquiri
Susan Thompson, Scottville

1 can (6 oz.) frozen limeade or lemonade
25 large, fresh strawberries, hulled and washed
2 T. sugar
1-1/2 cups light rum
3 cups ice cubes

In a blender, place all ingredients. Pulse and blend until desired consistency. Pour into pitcher over ice cubes and serve. Yield: 8-12 servings.

Kale & Quinoa Salad, page 45

SALADS, SOUPS & SIDE DISHES

Asian Chicken Salad

Mary Cooper-Nichols, Ludington

1 pkg. frozen, breaded chicken breast meat (prefer honey/bbq)
1 head green cabbage, shaved/chopped
2 carrots, shaved/chopped
2 celery stalks, sliced/chopped
1 small onion, chopped

Asian Dressing
1/2 cup apple cider vinegar
1/2 cup white sugar
1/4 cup honey teriyaki marinade
1 T. sesame oil
2 T. maple syrup
1 tsp. salt
1 tsp. pepper
1/2 tsp. seasoned salt
Sunflower and pumpkin seeds

Prepare chicken in oven per directions on package. Allow to cool and cut into bite size pieces. Put all shaved/chopped vegetables in a large bowl. Chill in refrigerator.

For the dressing: In a saucepan, combine all ingredients except seeds and bring to a boil. Let cool.

Drizzle dressing over salad, and toss JUST BEFORE SERVING. Top with chicken and sprinkle with sunflower seeds and pumpkin seeds. Yield: 4 servings.

The sweet-and-tangy dressing is the hero of this salad. It may not be authentically Asian, but I can attest that it's authentically delicious.

Light and refreshing, this shrimp salad is a low-muss, low-fuss choice for a hot summer day when you'd rather be doing anything else but cooking.

Summer Shrimp Salad

Maxine Wagner, Ludington

1 head iceberg lettuce, thinly sliced
1 bag (8-12 oz.) frozen salad shrimp, thawed and drained
1/4 cup onion, minced or diced
1/4 cup celery, diced
2-3 hard-boiled eggs, sliced
3/4 cup whipped salad dressing
1 T. horseradish sauce
1/3 cup milk
Salt and pepper to taste

In large bowl, toss lettuce, shrimp, onion, celery and egg. In small bowl, mix salad dressing, horseradish sauce, milk, salt and pepper until blended. Pour over the salad and toss until well-coated. Serve immediately. Yield: 2-4 servings.

Broccoli Salad

Arlene Quick, Scottville

2 medium size heads of broccoli, cut in bite-sized pieces (can also use cauliflower pieces)
1 can (8 oz.) water chestnuts, cut in pieces
1/4 cup red onion, diced
4-6 slices of crisp bacon, crumbled
1/2 cup cashews, chopped
1/2 cup dried cranberries, chopped coarsely
1 cup mayonnaise
1/2 cup sugar

In large bowl, mix broccoli, water chestnuts, onion, bacon, cashews and cranberries. In small bowl, mix mayonnaise and sugar and pour over the broccoli salad. Mix until throughly coated. Yield: 10 servings.

Three Bean Salad

Maxine Wagner, Ludington

1 can (14.5 oz.) green beans, drained
1 can (14.5 oz.) yellow beans, drained
1 can (14.5 oz.) red kidney beans, drained
1/2 cup green pepper, diced
1/3 cup red pepper, diced
1/3 cup red onion, diced
1 jar (4 oz.) diced pimentos (opt.)
1/2 cup celery, diced
2/3 cup apple cider vinegar
1/2 cup vegetable oil
1/2 cup sugar
1 tsp. Worcestershire sauce
1/2 tsp. pepper
1/2 tsp. salt
1/2 tsp garlic, crushed
1/2 tsp. celery seed

In large bowl, mix beans, peppers, onion, pimentos and celery. In separate bowl, mix all other ingredients until blended. Pour over the bean mixture. Toss gently. Cover and store in refrigerator overnight. Yield: 8-10 servings.

Spinach Salad

Maxine Wagner, Ludington

1/2 cup vegetable oil
1/4 cup ketchup
1/4 cup white vinegar
1 tsp. Worcestershire sauce
2 T. sugar
1 tsp. salt
1/4 tsp. pepper
1 lb. fresh spinach
4-5 slices crisp bacon, crumbled
2 hard-boiled eggs, chopped or sliced
5-6 fresh mushrooms, sliced
Red onion, thinly sliced

In a blender, combine oil, ketchup, vinegar, Worcestershire sauce, sugar, salt and pepper. Refrigerate. In large bowl, combine spinach, bacon, eggs, mushrooms and onion. Pour dressing over salad and toss. Yield: 4 servings.

Bacon makes everything better, including vegetables. Plus, it's low fat – it goes right to your lower waist.

Each of these robust salads pairs perfectly with grilled meats, so they make great side dishes for summer picnics.

Spinach Pear Salad

Greg Wagner, Caledonia

4 T. vegetable oil
3 T. white wine vinegar
1/4 cup sugar
4 T. mayonnaise
1/8 tsp. each salt, pepper and garlic salt
1 pkg. (10 oz.) fresh leaf spinach
1-2 ripe pears, cored and sliced
Crumbled gorgonzola or blue cheese

In a small bowl, whisk together vegetable oil, vinegar, sugar, mayonnaise, salt, pepper and garlic salt. In large bowl, toss spinach and pears. Pour desired amout of dressing over the spinach, add cheese and toss until coated. Yield: 4 servings.

Macaroni Salad

Maxine Wagner, Ludington

1 pkg. (16 oz.) elbow macaroni
1/2 cup white onion, diced
1/2 cup celery, diced
2 small tomatoes, diced
1 small cucumber, sliced and quartered

Sauce
1 cup whipped salad dressing
1 T. horseradish sauce
1/3 cup milk
2 T. sugar
Salt and pepper to taste

Cook macaroni according to package directions. Rinse in cold water and drain well. Mix in all other vegetables. In a small bowl, whisk salad dressing, horseradish sauce, milk, sugar, salt and pepper. Pour dressing over salad and toss. Refrigerate. Cold, cooked shrimp or crab are nice additions. Yield: 16-20 servings.

Crunchy Romaine Toss

Kathy Wagner, Caledonia

My wife Kathy's romaine salad can be tossed together at the drop of a hat – ideal for impromptu beach trips.

1/4 cup butter
1 (3 oz.) pkg. ramen noodles
1 cup walnuts, chopped
1/2 cup olive oil
1/4 cup honey
1/3 cup white wine vinegar
1/4 tsp. salt
1/4 tsp. pepper
1 lb. fresh broccoli, chopped
1 head romaine, torn in small pieces
4 green onions, sliced

Preheat oven to 350°. Discard ramen seasoning packet. In baking pan, melt butter. Break noodles into small pieces and place in the buttered pan with walnuts. Bake for 10 minutes until gently browned, stirring occasionally. Let cool. In large bowl, whisk olive oil, honey, vinegar, salt and pepper. Add ramen/walnut mixture, broccoli, lettuce and green onion. Toss to coat. Yield: 6 servings.

Ramen noodles add a fun twist to this crisp and crunchy salad. The robust cabbage resists wilting, so it's great for gatherings of any type.

Napa Cabbage Salad

Doris Hartman, Ludington

1 stick butter or margarine
2 pkgs. (3 oz.) ramen noodles broken in small pieces
1/2 cup sesame seeds
1 pkg. (2.1 oz.) slivered or sliced almonds
1 large head Napa cabbage, chopped fine
5 green onions, sliced
1 cup carrots, shredded
1 T. cilantro, chopped

Dressing
1 cup vegetable oil
1 tsp. sesame oil
2 tsp. soy sauce
1 cup sugar
1/2 cup white vinegar

Discard the ramen seasoning packet. In fry pan, melt butter and brown noodles, sesame seeds and almonds. Drain on paper towels and set aside. In large bowl, place cabbage, onions, carrots and cilantro.

For the dressing: Mix all ingredients in small bowl until blended. Drizzle dressing over salad and toss. It is best served immediately.
Yield: 8-10 servings.

Summer Salad

Kathy Wagner, Caledonia

1 cup slivered almonds
1/3 cup sugar
1 lb. spring mix greens
1/2 cup dried cranberries or tart cherries
1 box (16 oz.) strawberries, washed and sliced
3 kiwis, peeled and sliced
1 ripe mango, peeled and diced
1/4 cup red wine vinegar
1/2 cup olive oil
1/2 cup sugar
3/4 tsp. salt

In a small pan, heat almonds and sugar over low heat, stirring constantly until sugar melts. Remove from heat and let cool. In large salad bowl, toss greens, cranberries, strawberries, kiwi and mango. In a small bowl, whisk together vinegar, oil, sugar and salt until blended. Pour over salad and toss gently. Top with sugared almonds. Yield: 10 servings.

Michigan's strawberry season is not long, but it is spectacular. I use them anywhere I can – including salads.

Esquites (Corn) Salad

Kelly Green, Caledonia

2 cans (15 oz.) corn
3/4 cup red pepper, diced
3/4 cup yellow pepper, diced
4 green onions, sliced
2 cups (8 oz. pkg.) shredded cheese, (cheddar, Colby, etc.)
1 cup mayonnaise
1 bag (9.25 oz.) chili cheese corn chips, broken in pieces

In a salad bowl, mix all ingredients except corn chips together. Refrigerate for at least 1 hour. Just before serving, mix in corn chips. Yield: 10 servings.

Frozen corn makes this recipe super easy but every once in awhile I make it with fresh Michigan sweet corn – so crisp and juicy!

Bean & Corn Salad

Greg Wagner, Caledonia

- 2 can (15 oz.) black beans, drained and rinsed
- 2 cups frozen corn, thawed
- 1 small red onion, diced
- 1 red pepper, diced
- 1/2 cup vegetable oil
- 1/2 cup red wine vinegar
- 1/3 cup sugar
- 1 tsp. cumin
- 1/2 tsp. garlic powder
- Salt and pepper to taste
- 3 T. cilantro, chopped
- 1-2 limes, juiced

In salad bowl combine all ingredients and mix well. Refrigerate. Serve as a side salad but also great as a taco chip dip. Yield: 8-10 servings.

Kale & Quinoa Salad

Greg Wagner, Caledonia

- 3 cups quinoa, cooked (1 cup uncooked) and chilled
- 10 leaves of fresh kale, chopped fine
- 1 cup pecans, chopped and toasted
- 1 cup dried cranberries, chopped
- 1/4 cup olive oil
- 3 T. lemon juice
- 1 tsp. Dijon mustard
- 1 garlic clove, minced
- 1/2 tsp. black pepper
- 1/2 tsp. salt
- 2 T. sugar
- 3/4 cup feta cheese, crumbled

In salad bowl, combine quinoa, kale, pecans and cranberries, and mix well. In a small bowl, whisk olive oil, lemon juice, mustard, garlic, pepper, salt and sugar. Pour dressing over the salad and toss until well coated. Fold in the feta and refrigerate. Yield: 8-10 servings.

Friends don't let friends serve bad salads. My pal Lisa has never steered me wrong!

Greek Spinach Pasta Salad

Lisa Ziemke, Caledonia

1 pkg. (16 oz.) penne pasta, cooked according to package
1 pkg. (10 oz.) fresh spinach
1 can (3.8 oz.) sliced black olives
1 pint sweet grape tomatoes, halved
Greek salad dressing
Feta cheese crumbles

In a large salad bowl, toss pasta, spinach, olives and tomatoes. Apply as much dressing as preferred and toss gently. Add feta cheese as much as desired. Yield: 10-12 servings.

7-Layer Salad

Maxine Wagner, Ludington

1 head iceberg lettuce, washed and shredded
10 green onions, sliced
1 pkg. (12 oz.) frozen peas, (microwave 1-2 minutes & drain)
4 strips crisp bacon, crumbled
5 hard-boiled eggs, sliced
2 cups mayonnaise
1 T. sugar
1 pkg. (8 oz.) shredded cheddar cheese

In a 13" x 9" glass dish, layer lettuce, onions, peas, bacon and eggs. In a small bowl, blend mayonnaise and sugar and spread over the salad. Sprinkle cheese over the top. Refrigerate. Yield: 12-15 servings.

This is Mom's interpretation of classic German potato salad, which became a family favorite and is still served in Wagner households across the state.

Classic Potato Salad

Maxine Wagner, Ludington

3 lb. bag Yellow or Russet potatoes, peeled, boiled and sliced in pieces
1 small yellow onion, diced
4 stalks celery, diced
6 hard-boiled eggs, sliced
4-6 radishes, sliced thin

Sauce
1-1/2 cups whipped salad dressing
2-3 T. yellow mustard
1 T. horseradish sauce
1/2 cup milk
2 T. sugar
1 tsp. celery seed
Salt and pepper to taste

In large salad bowl, place potatoes, onion, celery, eggs and radishes. In a small bowl, whisk salad dressing, mustard, horseradish sauce, milk, sugar, celery seed, salt and pepper. Pour dressing over potatoes and toss until well coated. Refrigerate. Yield: 8-10 servings.

"Fast Food" Burger Salad

Susan Thompson, Scottville

3/4 cup mayonnaise
4 tsp. yellow mustard
2 T. dill pickles, chopped
1 T. onion, chopped
1 T. white vinegar
2 tsp. sugar
1/2 tsp. paprika
1 lb. ground beef or turkey
1 tsp. salt
1 tsp. pepper
4 cups iceberg or romaine lettuce, chopped
1/2 cup onions, sliced thin and halved
1 cup shredded cheddar cheese
1/4 cup dill pickles, chopped

In a small bowl, mix mayonnaise, mustard, pickles, onion, vinegar, sugar and paprika. In frying pan, brown meat, add salt and pepper. In a salad bowl, combine lettuce, onions, shredded cheese and remaining pickles. Into 4 bowls, place equal amounts of the lettuce mixture. Then top with equal amounts of the meat.. Drizzle with dressing and serve immediately. Yield: 4 servings.

Thousand Island Dressing

Sue Siler, Alto

2 cups mayonnaise
1/8 cup green pepper, chopped fine
1/4 cup sweet onion, chopped fine
1-1/2 tsp. dried parsley
3 T. ketchup
1/8 cup sugar
1/4 cup sour cream

In a mixing bowl, beat together all ingredients well. Refrigerate. Yield: 20-24 servings.

French Dressing

Lynn Schumacher, Caledonia

1 cup mayonnaise
1 T. ketchup, heaping
2 T. vinegar
1 T. milk
1 tsp. paprika
1/2 tsp. dry mustard

In a mixing bowl, beat all ingredients well. Refrigerate. Yield: 8-10 servings.

Ruby French Dressing

Lynn Schumacher, Caledonia

1/3 cup vegetable oil
1/4 cup ketchup
3 T. vinegar
2 T. onion, chopped fine
1 tsp. lemon juice
1/4 tsp. salt
1/4 tsp. pepper
1/4 tsp. dry mustard
1/4 tsp. paprika

In a large jar, mix all ingredients and shake well. Refrigerate. Yield: 8-10 servings.

Top your fresh summer salads with fresh-made dressings – easy and much more flavorful than store-bought versions.

Dressed to thrill: this zesty lime & garlic vinaigrette pairs well with both vegetables and fruits.

Vinaigrette Dressing

Maxine Wagner, Ludington

1/4 cup vegetable oil
1/3 cup white wine vinegar
1 T. parsley, snipped
1 tsp. Worcestershire sauce
1/2 tsp. salt
1/4 tsp. dry mustard
1/4 tsp. ground pepper
1 clove garlic, crushed

Combine all ingredients in a jar and shake until blended. Refrigerate. Yield: 3/4 cup.

Lime & Garlic Dressing

Greg Wagner, Caledonia

1/2 cup olive oil
1/3 cup white wine vinegar
1 lime, juiced
2 T. sugar
1/2 tsp. salt
1/4 tsp. ground pepper
1 clove garlic, crushed

Combine all ingredients in a jar and shake until blended. Refrigerate. Yield: 3/4 cup.

Aunt Ve's Gelatin Salad

Vera VanDyke, Ludington

Gelatin
- 3 pkgs. (3 oz.) gelatin, 2 lemon and 1 lime
- 3 cups hot water
- 3 cups lemon-lime soft drink
- 1 can (11 oz.) mandarin oranges, drained
- 1 can (20 oz.) crushed pineapple (reserve juice for topping)
- 1/2 cup halved maraschino cherries
- 3-4 ripe bananas
- 1 bag (16 oz.) mini marshmallows

Topping
- 1 cup pineapple juice
- 1 T. butter
- 1/2 cup sugar
- 2 T. flour
- 1 egg, beaten
- 1 cup heavy whipping cream
- 1/4 cup chopped pecans (optional)

Dissolve gelatin in hot water. Add soft drink, oranges, pineapple and maraschino cherries. Pour mixture into glass 15" x 10" and 8" x 8" glass baking dishes (makes enough for two salads). Refrigerate until slightly thick. Stir so the fruit floats and is not just at the bottom. Top with sliced bananas and mini marshmallows. Chill until firm. Spread topping. Chill.

For the topping. Heat pineapple juice, butter and sugar. Whisk in flour and egg. Cook on low heat until thick and bubbly. Cool completely.

In small bowl, whip cream until it forms soft peaks. Do not over beat. Fold whipping cream and pineapple mixture together until blended. Spread over the chilled gelatin. Garnish with chopped pecans, if desired. Yield: 24 servings.

It just wasn't a party until Aunt Ve arrived with this fruit-filled favorite. We carry on her tradition at today's family gatherings!

My sister-in-law Judy puts the jiggle in dessert with this rainbow delight.

7-Layer Gelatin

Judy Wagner, Ludington

2 cups milk
1 cup sugar
2 envelopes unflavored gelatin
1/2 cup cold water
2 cups sour cream
2 tsp. vanilla extract
4 pkgs. (3 oz.) gelatin
   (any 4 flavors)
4 cups boiling water

For the white layer, bring milk to boil in a saucepan. Stir in sugar. Remove from heat. In separate bowl, dissolve unflavored gelatin in cold water. Add unflavored gelatin, sour cream and vanilla to milk mixture and blend well with whisk until creamy. Set aside. Dissolve one package of gelatin in 1 cup boiling water. Repeat with the other 3 flavors of gelatin and set aside. Pour first layer of gelatin in a 13" x 9" glass dish. Refrigerate until firm (make sure the dish is level). Add approximately 1-1/2 cups of white gelatin mixture on top of the first gelatin layer. Chill until firm. Add the next layer of gelatin on top of the white layer. Pour gelatin onto a spoon so the gelatin flows evenly over the white layer. Chill until firm. Repeat these steps until the last layer of gelatin is applied. Chill until firm. With a sharp knife, cut into squares and serve. Yield: 24 servings.

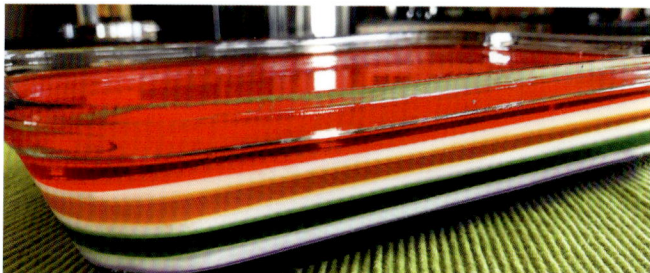

Raspberry-Cranberry Gelatin

June Strahan, Ludington

2 pkgs. (6 oz.) raspberry gelatin
1 cup boiling water
1-1/2 cup cold water
1 can (20 oz.) crushed pineapple
   (reserve juice for topping)
1 can (14 oz.) cranberry sauce
1 orange cut in small pieces
1/2 cup chopped walnuts
1/3 cup mayonnaise
1/4 cup pineapple juice

Dissolve gelatin in 1 cup boiling water. Add cold water and stir. Stir in pineapple, cranberry sauce, orange and walnuts. Pour into gelatin mold. Chill until firm. Remove gelatin from mold and place on serving plate. Blend mayonnaise and pineapple juice and drizzle over the gelatin. Yield: 12 servings.

Easy Chili

Karen Rambo, Washington Courthouse, Ohio

1 to 2 lbs. ground beef or turkey
1 jar (16 oz.) salsa (choose your heat preference)
1 can (15 oz.) black beans, drained and rinsed
1 can (15 oz.) pinto or kidney beans, drained and rinsed
1 can (15 oz.) corn, drained
2 cans (15 oz.) diced tomatoes
1 T. cocoa powder

In soup pot, brown meat. Add all ingredients and simmer for 30 minutes.
Yield: 6 servings.

Hearty Veggie Soup

Greg Wagner, Caledonia

1 box (32 oz.) veggie broth
2 cups water
1 onion, diced
4 stalks celery, sliced
4 carrots, sliced
1 can (15 oz.) black beans, pinto, kidney or garbanzo beans, drained and rinsed
1 can (15 oz.) corn, drained
2 cans (15 oz.) diced tomatoes
1/2 cup quinoa, uncooked
1 T. chili powder
1 tsp. garlic powder
2 tsp. cumin
1 tsp. salt
1/2 tsp. pepper
1/3 cup cilantro, chopped

In large soup pot, add all ingredients and simmer for 30 minutes.
Yield: 10 servings.

We meet up with neighbors to feast on this shrimp chowder before going to church together every Christmas Eve.

Shrimp Chowder

Cheryl Blanchard, Caledonia

3 pkgs. (8 oz.) cream cheese
5 cans milk (use soup can)
2 T. butter
1 bunch green onions, sliced
2 cloves garlic, minced
1 lb. peeled shrimp, uncooked
5 cans (10.5 oz.) cream of potato soup
1 tsp. cayenne pepper
1 (15 oz.) can corn, undrained

Cut cream cheese into cubes and combine with 1/2 of the milk in a large pot, stirring until cheese is melted. Meanwhile, in a large pan, melt butter and sauté chopped onion and garlic. Add soup and cayenne pepper and simmer. Pour into the pot and add the rest of the milk, shrimp and undrained corn. Heat together, but don't boil. Yield: 6-8 servings.

Chicken Noodle Soup

David Driscoll, Caledonia

1/2 cup (1 stick) salted butter
5 cloves garlic, minced
1 medium-large onion, diced
1 cup celery, diced
1-2 cups carrots, sliced
1 tsp. black pepper
2 tsp. thyme
1/2 tsp. crushed rosemary
1/2 tsp. sage
1 rotisserie chicken, deboned and torn in small pieces
2 cans (49.5 oz.) chicken broth
1 cup frozen peas
1 cup frozen corn
1 pkg. (16 oz.) Kluski noodles*

*Optional Homemade Noodles
1 cup all-purpose flour
1 tsp. salt
1 egg, beaten
1 T. cold water or enough to make a stiff dough

In a large pot, melt butter. Add garlic, onions, celery and carrots, and sauté for 5-8 minutes. Add pepper, thyme, rosemary, sage and chicken bits to sauté. Add chicken broth, peas and corn, and bring to a boil. Add noodles and boil for 16-18 minutes. Yield: 10-12 servings.

For optional homemade noodles: In a small bowl, mix ingredients well and roll out thin on a lightly floured surface. Cut noodles as wide and long as desired. Drop into simmering broth.

White Reaper Chicken Chili
Meagan Draper, Greenville

- 1 can (15 oz.) corn
- 1 can (15.5 oz.) Great Northern beans, drained
- 1 rottiserie chicken, deboned and torn in bite size pieces
- 3 cups chicken broth
- 2-3 T. all-purpose flour
- 2 T. onions, minced
- 3 T garlic, minced
- 1 tsp. chili powder
- 2 T. salt
- 2 T. pepper
- 2 cups shredded Co-jack cheese
- 1 dried Carolina whole reaper pepper (very hot!); a milder pepper can be substituted if desired
- 1 tsp. ground ginger
- 1 tsp. dry mustard
- 1 cup half-and-half
- 1 avocado, thin slices
- 1/2 cup fresh basil, chopped

In a slow cooker, add all ingredients except for the cheese and half and half. Cook for 10 hours on low. 30 minutes prior to serving, blend in cheese and half-and-half. More flour or cheese can be added for desired thickness. Top with sliced avocado and basil leaves. Yield: 12 servings.

Not for the faint of heart! This spicy chili won first place in a Detroit chili cook-off. Keep water handy.

Cabbage Bean Soup
Susan Thompson, Scottville

- 1-2 T. vegetable oil
- 1/2 cup onion, diced
- 2 cups water
- 6 oz. pre-cooked ham, diced
- 2 cups cabbage, shredded
- 2 cans (14.5 oz.) diced tomatoes
- 1 tsp. chili powder
- 1/4 tsp. pepper
- 1 can (15.5 oz.) Great Northern beans, drained

In a large soup pot, sauté onion in oil until tender. Add water, ham, cabbage, tomatoes and seasonings. Bring to boil. Lower heat, cover and simmer for 15 minutes. Add beans. Continue simmering for 20 minutes. Yield: 8-10 servings.

Another traditional German dish – though I'm pretty sure the cream of mushroom soup is an American addition.

Potato-Sauerkraut Soup

Susan Thompson, Scottville

- 4 cups chicken broth
- 5 cans (10.5 oz.) cream of mushroom soup
- 1 jar (16 oz.) sauerkraut, drained and rinsed
- 8 oz. mushrooms (fresh or canned), sliced
- 1 medium potato, cubed
- 2 medium carrots, sliced
- 1 medium onion, diced
- 2 stalks celery, diced
- 3/4 lb. smoked sausage, cubed
- 1/2 cup cooked chicken, cubed
- 2 T. vinegar
- 2 tsp. dried dill weed
- 1/2 tsp. pepper
- 2 slices of crisp bacon, crumbled

In a large slow cooker, stir together all ingredients except bacon. Cover and cook on low heat setting for 10 to 12 hours. Sprinkle each serving with bacon. Yield: 6-8 servings.

Easy White Chicken Chili

Tracy Wagner, Pentwater

- 1 can (48 oz.) deluxe mixed beans, drained
- 1 can (12 oz.) chicken
- 1 tsp. cumin
- 1 pkg. (8 oz.) shredded Colby cheese
- 1 jar (16 oz.) salsa
- 1/2 cup onion, chopped

In a large slow cooker, stir together all ingredients. Cover and cook on low heat setting for 2-4 hours. Yield: 6-8 servings.

Turkey Barley Soup

Jeff Wagner, Pentwater

- 1 lb. ground turkey
- 1 T. olive oil
- 1 small onion, chopped
- 1 tsp. garlic, minced
- 5 cups water
- 1 can (16 oz.) diced tomatoes
- 1/3 cup pearl barley
- 1/4 cup ketchup
- 1 T. beef boullion
- 1 tsp. dried basil
- 1-2 bay leaves
- 1 bag (16 oz.) frozen mixed vegetables

In a soup pot, brown turkey with olive oil. Then add onions and garlic, and sauté for 2 minutes. Add water and the rest of the ingredients except for the frozen vegetables. Bring to boil then simmer on low heat for about 45 minutes. Take out bay leaves, add frozen vegetables and cook for about 10 minutes. Yield: 6-8 servings.

Good Ol' Chili

Maxine Wagner, Ludington

- 2 lbs. ground beef or turkey
- 1 onion, diced
- 4 stalks celery, diced
- 2 gloves garlic, minced
- 3 cans (14.5 oz.) diced tomatoes
- 1 can (15 oz.) tomato sauce
- 1/2 cup water
- 2-1/2 T. chili powder
- 1 tsp dried oregano leaves
- 1 tsp. salt
- 1 tsp. pepper
- 2 cans (15 oz.) beans (kidney, pinto, black, etc.), drained and rinsed
- 1 can (15 oz.) corn, drained (opt.)

In a large pot, brown meat. Add onions, celery and garlic and sauté for 5 minutes. Add tomatoes, tomato sauce, water, chili powder, oregano, salt and pepper. Cook on low heat for about an hour. Add beans and cook for about 10 minutes. Serve with sour cream and shredded cheddar cheese. Yield: 6-8 servings.

These robust and hearty soups are worthy of entrée status. Slurp on!

My brother Ed doesn't care that mulligatawny is a fusion of Indian and British cuisine — all that matters to him is that it tastes good. (And it does!)

Broccoli Cauliflower Soup
Mary Cooper-Nichols, Ludington

2 heads and stems fresh broccoli, cut in pieces
1 cauliflower head, cut in pieces
4 large carrots, chunked
1 medium onion, chopped
2 stalks celery, diced
1 qt. water or vegetable stock
1/4 cup butter
1/4 cup all-purpose flour
3-4 cups milk
1/2 tsp. salt
1/2 tsp. pepper
1 cup soft cheese loaf, cubed
1/2 cup (1 stick) butter

In a soup pot, place all vegetables and water or stock. Bring to a boil, reduce heat and cook until vegetables are tender. Remove from heat. Use an immersion blender or chop/mash fine to puree the vegetable mixture. Return to stove top on low heat. In a separate pan, make a blond roux with the butter and flour by melting the butter and whisking in the flour on medium heat. Gradually add the milk, salt and pepper until thickened. Add the roux mixture to the vegetable puree. While this mixture simmers, add the cheese and remaining butter. Use the immersion blender or mash again to blend. More milk can be added for a thinner soup. Taste for seasoning and sprinkle with parsley flakes. Simmer for 15 minutes and serve with croutons. Variations: Reserve some broccoli and cauliflower pieces for a chunkier soup. Add a slight sprinkle of cayenne pepper for a little heat. Yield: 6-8 servings.

Mulligatawny Soup
Ed Wagner, Ludington

2 large carrots, chopped
1 medium onion, chopped
2 stalks celery, diced
2 cloves garlic, minced
1/2 lb. chicken, uncooked and cubed
1 T. curry powder
1 tsp. cumin
Salt and pepper to taste
1 container (32 oz.) chicken stock
1/2 cup jasmine rice, rinsed and uncooked.
1 can (13.5 oz.) coconut milk

In a fry pan, sauté carrots, onion, celery and garlic until tender. Set aside. In a stock pot, brown chicken until done. Add the vegetable mixture. Add curry powder, cumin, salt and pepper. Add chicken stock and rice and simmer for about an hour. Add coconut milk and simmer an additional 10 minutes. Serve with chopped cashews and cilantro, if desired. Yield: 4-6 servings.

Minestrone Milano Soup
Sue Siler, Alto

2 T. olive oil
1 lb. ground turkey sausage
6 cups beef broth
1 clove garlic, minced
1-1/2 tsp. dried basil
1-1/2 tsp. dried oregano
2 cans (28 oz.) diced tomatoes
2 cups cabbage, chopped
1 cup celery, chopped
1 cup onion, chopped
1 cup carrot, chopped
1 cup frozen peas
1 cup fresh or frozen spinach, chopped
2 small zucchinis, chopped
2 cups pasta shells, cooked

In a soup pot, brown turkey sausage in olive oil. Add the broth, garlic, seasonings and tomatoes, and bring to a boil. Reduce heat and simmer for 30 minutes. Then add all other ingredients except for the pasta and simmer until vegetables are tender. Add some cooked pasta shells to individual bowls. a dash of red pepper can be added for a little zip. Yield: 10-12 servings.

Seafood Chowder
Mary Cooper-Nichols, Ludington

4 crab legs
1 bag frozen shrimp (shells on)
2 cups water
1 stick butter
1 lb. frozen cod
1 pkg. frozen clams (can use canned)
2 T. butter
1 carrot, peeled
1 medium onion
2 stalks celery
1/4 cup butter
1/4 cup all-purpose flour
Salt and pepper to taste
4 cups milk
1 tsp. thyme
1-2 T. parsley flakes

Place the crab legs and shrimp in a shallow pan, add 2 cups of water and 1 stick of butter. Place cover on pan and steam 4-5 minutes. Remove from heat and strain liquid from the pan. Save the liquid and place in soup stock pot. Peel the shrimp and crab and cut shrimp in half. Place in stock pot and set aside. In a blender, chop carrot, onion and celery. In shallow pan, add 2 T. butter and sauté the chopped vegetables until tender (5-7 minutes). Place the sautéed vegetables in the soup stock pot. In a saucepan, make a roux by adding butter, flour, salt, pepper and milk. Cook until thickened and add thyme. Pour roux into the stock pot. Place the pot on the stovetop on medium heat. Add the remaining cod and clams to the soup and allow to simmer for about 1 hour. Add parsley flakes and stir. Serve with homemade croutons or bruschetta. Add a splash of hot sauce (opt.) Yield: 10-12 servings.

My cousins Sue and Mary (and their sister Jeri) are spectacular cooks. I'm so happy to share their best recipes in this book.

You could feed an army with this recipe (or at least a platoon). Make the whole batch and refrigerate the leftovers, it'll taste even better the next day.

Meatball Minestrone Soup

Sue Siler, Alto

1 cup celery, diced
1 cup onion, diced
1 clove garlic, minced
2 T. vegetable oil
1 can (14.5 oz.) diced tomatoes
1 can (6 oz.) tomato paste
4 qts. water
1 tsp. salt
1 tsp. dried oregano
1/2 tsp. dried basil
1-1/2 lbs. ground beef or turkey
3/4 cup bread crumbs
1/2 cup grated parmesan cheese
2 T. dried parsley flakes
2 eggs
1 small onion, minced
1 clove garlic, minced
2 tsp. salt
1/2 tsp. pepper
1 can (15 oz.) each of baked, red kidney and garbanzo beans, undrained
1 pkg. (8 oz.) fresh spinach
1 carrot, sliced
2 tsp. fresh parsley, chopped
1/2 pkg. (8 oz.) thin spaghetti, broken in 2" pieces, cooked and drained

In a soup pot, sauté celery, onion and garlic in oil. Add tomatoes, tomato paste, water, salt, oregano and basil. Cook to boiling. In a large bowl, throughly mix ground beef or turkey, bread crumbs, parmesan cheese, parsley flakes, eggs, onion, garlic, salt and pepper. Shape into small 1" balls. Add to boiling soup. Lower heat and simmer for 30 minutes. Add beans, spinach, carrot and parsley. Cover and simmer for 30 minutes. Add pasta and heat through and serve. Soup may be frozen. Yield: 14-16 servings.

Glorified Rice

Maxine Wagner, Ludington

1 can (20 oz.) crushed pineapple, with juice
1/2 cup sugar
1 T. cornstarch
1/2 tsp. salt
5-6 cups cooked white rice
1 can (11 oz.) of mandarin oranges, halved
1/2 cup maraschino cherries, halved
2 cups mini marshmallows (opt.)
1 tub (8 oz.) whipped topping

In saucepan, combine pineapple with juice, sugar, cornstarch and salt. Bring to a boil, stirring constantly until mixture thickens. Cool. In large bowl, mix rice, oranges, cherries and marshmallows (opt.) Pour cooked pineapple into rice and stir. Fold in whipped topping. Chill. Yield: 16-20 servings.

Hot German Potato Salad

Maxine Wagner, Ludington

6 potatoes, boiled and sliced
6 pieces of crisp bacon, broken in pieces (reserve drippings)
3/4 cup onion, diced
3/4 cup celery, diced
2 T. all-purpose flour
2 T. sugar
1-1/2 tsp. salt
Dash of pepper
3/4 cup water
1/3 cup white vinegar

In large bowl, place sliced potatoes and fried bacon pieces. In large fry pan, sauté onions and celery in bacon drippings until golden brown. Blend in flour, sugar, salt and pepper, and cook over low heat until smooth and bubbly. Remove from heat and stir in water and vinegar. Bring to boil, stirring constantly. Boil 1 minute. Gently mix in potatoes and bacon and heat until warm. Serve warm. Yield: 8-10 servings.

Mom's glorified rice recipe is a bit more complex than others, but it's worth the extra effort. It was a mainstay of graduation parties and holiday dinners.

Two hash brown casseroles: one fattening and the other REALLY fattening. Both are delicious, so you can't go wrong either way.

Cheesy Potatoes
Sue Siler, Alto

- 1 pkg. (28-32 oz.) frozen hash brown potatoes
- 1-1/2 cups light mayonnaise
- 1-1/2 cups shredded sharp cheddar cheese
- 2 T. onion, finely chopped

In a large bowl, combine all ingredients and mix well. Spread mixture in a well-greased 13" x 9" pan. Bake at 350° for 1 hour. Yield: 6-8 servings.

Potato Casserole
Deanna Dorff, Mt. Morris

- 1 pkg. (28-32 oz.) frozen hash brown potatoes
- 1 can (10.5 oz.) cream of chicken soup
- 1 cup sour cream
- 1 pkg. (8 oz.) shredded sharp cheddar cheese
- 1/2 cup onion, finely chopped
- 4 T. butter or margarine
- 1 cup cheese crackers, crushed

In a large bowl, combine potatoes, soup, sour cream, cheese and onion, and mix well. Melt butter in the bottom of a 13" x 9" pan. Spread potato mixture into the pan. Cover with cheese crackers. Bake at 350° for 45-50 minutes. Yield: 6-8 servings.

Baked Beans

Ruth Ann Dittmer, Ludington

- 3 cans (15.5 oz.) Great Northern beans, drained
- 1/2 cup molasses
- 1 T. vinegar
- 1/2 cup brown sugar
- 1/2 cup water
- 1/2 cup ketchup
- 1-1/2 tsp. dry mustard
- 1 large onion, diced
- 4-5 bacon strips, cut in small pieces, partially cooked

- Preheat oven to 350°.
- Combine all ingredients in baking pan, including bacon and drippings; mix well. Bake 1 to 1-1/2 hours.
- Yield: 16-18 servings.

Tomato Pie

Greg Wagner, Caledonia

- 1 (9") pie crust, baked
- 1 egg white, slightly beaten
- 3-4 tomatoes, peeled and sliced
- 1/2 cup mayonnaise
- 1/4 cup grated parmesan cheese, divided
- 1/8 tsp. dry mustard
- 1 tsp. lemon juice
- 1/2 tsp. fresh or 1/4 tsp. dried basil
- 1/8 tsp. cracked pepper
- 1/8 tsp. garlic powder

- Preheat oven to 350°. Brush crust with egg white and prick sides and bottom with tines of a fork. Bake for 10-12 minutes. Let crust cool. In a small bowl, mix mayonnaise, 3 T. parmesan cheese, mustard, lemon juice, basil, pepper and garlic powder. Lay tomatoes in the baked crust. Spoon mayonnaise mixture over the tomatoes and top with remaining cheese. Bake for 20 minutes or until top is golden brown.
- Yield: 4-6 servings.

There's nothing like the taste of tomatoes fresh from the garden. Here's a wonderful way to serve them in a side dish.

I was never a big fan of zucchini as a side dish ... until my wife smothered it in cheese and bread crumbs. (She knows the way to my heart.)

Baked Cheese Zucchini

Kathy Wagner, Caledonia

- 2 medium-sized zucchini, sliced
- 3 T. olive oil
- 1/2 cup panko bread crumbs
- 1/3 cup shredded parmesan cheese
- 1/4 tsp. garlic salt
- Fresh ground pepper

Preheat oven to 425°. In mixing bowl, toss all ingredients including zucchini. Place sliced zucchini on a greased, foil-lined baking sheet. Generously pile excess crumb/cheese mixture on top of each zucchini slice. Bake for 5-7 minutes or until cheese gets browned and crispy. Convection ovens work even better. Serve immediately. Yield: 4 servings.

Sweet & Sour Cabbage

Maxine Wagner, Ludington

- 3-4 bacon slices, cut into small pieces and fried crisp
- 2 onions, thinly sliced
- 4-6 cups shredded red cabbage
- 1/2 cup vinegar
- 1/2 cup water, grape or cranberry juice
- 2 T. sugar
- 2 tsp. salt
- Dash of paprika

In large fry pan, fry bacon pieces. Add onions and sauté for 5 minutes. Add remaining ingredients. Simmer for about an hour, stirring occasionally. Yield: 4-6 servings.

Sweet Potato Soufflé

Barb Greene, Akron, Ohio

4-5 sweet potatoes, baked, peeled and mashed
2 eggs, beaten
1 tsp. vanilla extract
2/3 cup sugar
1/2 cup (1 stick) butter
1/4 cup orange juice

Topping:
1 cup brown sugar
1/2 cup all-purpose flour
1/2 cup pecans, chopped
1/4 cup (1/2 stick) butter, melted

Preheat oven to 350°. In a large bowl, mix together potatoes, eggs, vanilla, sugar, butter and orange juice until smooth. Place in a greased baking dish.

For the topping: in small bowl, mix sugar, flour, pecans and melted butter. Sprinkle the topping over the potato mixture. Bake uncovered for 30-40 minutes. Yield: 6-8 servings.

It's a side dish! It's a dessert! It's a side dish and a dessert! My sister-in-law Barb has mastered this southern classic.

Wagner Mac 'n Cheese

Maxine Wagner, Ludington

1 lb. box favorite macaroni, rotini, shells or farfalle pasta, cooked and drained (reserve 1/2 cup pasta water)
4 oz. Swiss cheese
4 oz. Colby or Co-jack cheese
4 oz. sharp cheddar cheese
1 cup soft cheese loaf
2 cups milk
1/2 cup (1 stick) butter
Salt and pepper to taste

Preheat oven to 350°. In a large saucepan, combine all the cheeses, milk, butter, salt and pepper. Continue to stir until all the cheese is melted. Pour over the boiled, drained pasta. If additional liquid is needed, add a little of the reserved hot pasta water. Place in a well-buttered 13" x 9" glass casserole baking dish. Top with your favorite bread crumbs or pretzel dots. Yield: 8 servings.

With nine males in the house, Mom didn't think beans were such a magical fruit. But the taste of this dish was worth it!

Calico Beans

Mary Cooper-Nichols, Ludington

2 cans (28 oz.) of maple and bacon baked beans (drain juice only from one can)
1 can (15.8 oz.) each of great northern beans, dark red kidney beans, light red kidney beans, cannelli beans and pinto beans, drained
1 (8 oz.) can mushrooms, drained
1 lb. ground beef or turkey
1 large onion, chopped
1 lb. bacon, cooked and broken in pieces (reserve 2 T. drippings)
1/4 cup ketchup
1-1/2 T. yellow mustard
1/4 cup brown sugar
2 T. vinegar
Salt and pepper to taste

Preheat oven to 250° or use slow cooker. In a large bowl, combine all beans and mushrooms together. In a large pan, brown meat with onion. Drain any grease. Add reserved bacon drippings, bean mixture and bacon pieces. Then add ketchup, mustard, brown sugar, vinegar, salt and pepper. Place in slow cooker or baking pot. Cook or bake for 3-4 hours. Yield: 16-20 servings.

Cheesy Spaghetti Squash

Susan Thompson, Scottville

1 medium spaghetti squash
2-1/2 T. garlic, minced
1 tsp. olive oil
1 pkg. (5 oz.) fresh spinach, chopped
1/2 cup heavy cream
1 T. cream cheese
1/2 cup grated parmesan cheese
Sat and pepper to taste
Garnish of shredded mozzarella and grated parmesan cheese

Preheat oven to 400°. Pierce squash a few times and microwave 3-5 minutes to make cutting in half easier. Cut squash in half lengthwise and scoop out seeds. Brush the cut side of squash with olive oil. Place cut side down on a jelly roll pan. Bake for about 40 minutes. In fry pan, add olive oil and sauté garlic. Add spinach and cook until wilted. Add cream, parmesan cheese, salt and pepper. Stir well. Remove from heat. Once squash is done, use a fork to separate the strands. Pour spinach mixture over the squash strands and mix in the squash boat. Top with a little mozzarella and parmesan cheese. Bake for about 20 minutes. Yield: 2 servings.

Pistachio Bread, page 76

BREADS & BRUNCH

Bread Machine Rolls

Sara Petersen-Walunas, Ludington

1-1/2 cups warm water
3 T. butter, margarine or oil
1-1/2 tsp. salt
4-1/2 cups all-purpose flour
1/4 cup + 1 tsp. sugar
1/4 cup + 2 T. powdered milk
3 heaping tsp. active dry
   (or instant) yeast

Place ingredients in bread machine in order listed. Run on dough cycle. Shape into rolls as desired. Place in lightly greased pan, let rise until doubled. Bake at 350° for 15-20 minutes or until golden brown. Optional: brush tops of warm rolls with melted butter. Yield: 12-18 rolls.

White Bread

Jeanine Petersen, Ludington

3 cups warm water
3 T. active dry yeast
3 tsp. salt
3 T. vegetable oil
1/2 cup sugar
4 cups bread flour

In a large mixing bowl, combine water, yeast, salt, oil and sugar. Mix well. Let this dough rise until doubled. With dough hooks, gradually add bread flour. Knead with mixer until smooth. Place dough in a greased bowl, turning to coat. Cover with a damp cloth and let rise until doubled. Punch dough down and let rest a few minutes. Divide dough into 3 equal parts. Shape into loaves, place in greased loaf pans and let rise until almost doubled. (1-1/2" above the edge of the pan.) Bake at 350° for 35-40 minutes (cover with foil the last 15 minutes to prevent over-browning). Yield: 3 loaves.

These rolls were a staple at my second cousin Sara's Manitoba, Canada hunting lodge – Duck Mountain Outfitters. Now they're a staple at our tables.

Saturdays were baking days for my mom and my Aunt Helen. With 17 kids between them, it took all day to make bread and rolls for the week!

Butterflake Dinner Rolls

Helen Cooper, Ludington

1/2 cup milk, scalded
3 T. shortening
1/4 cup sugar
1/2 tsp. salt
1 pkg. active dry yeast dissolved in 1/2 cup warm water
1 egg, well beaten
1 egg yolk, well beaten
3 cups all-purpose flour
1 egg white, beaten
2 T. water
1/4 cup butter, softened

In a large bowl, combine milk, shortening, sugar and salt. Add yeast/water, egg, egg yolk and flour. Knead on a floured surface until smooth and elastic. Place in greased bowl and grease top of the dough. Cover and let rise until doubled in bulk (about 2 hours). Roll into a rectangle about 1/2" thick. Dot with butter. Fold in thirds to make three layers. Roll 1/2" thick and fold in thirds again. Cover and chill for 30 minutes. Roll dough 1/8" thick. Brush with melted butter and cut in 1/2" wide strips. Stack the strips 6 high. Cut the stacks in pieces 1-1/2" wide and place in greased muffin pans (cut edges up). Let rise until doubled in size. Brush with egg white mixed with 2 T. water. Bake at 425° for 15 minutes or until golden brown. Yield: 12 rolls.

Blue Cheese Rolls

Pat Keyser, Grand Rapids

4 T. butter, melted
1 pkg. (10 ct.) buttermilk biscuits
1 pkg. (4 oz.) bleu cheese, crumbled

Preheat oven to 400°. Melt the butter in an 8" x 8" baking dish. Sprinkle the bleu cheese over the melted butter. Remove biscuits from the package and roll them in the bleu cheese/butter mixture so there is bleu cheese on both sides of the biscuits. Place back in pan and bake for 8-10 minutes until golden brown. Yield: 10 rolls.

Crescent Rolls

Vera VanDyke, Ludington

3/4 cup milk
1/2 cup shortening
2 pkgs. active dry yeast
1/2 cup warm water
1/2 cup sugar
2 eggs, well beaten
1/2 tsp. salt
4 cups all-purpose flour
1/4 cup butter or margarine, melted

In saucepan, heat milk and shortening until melted. Cool to lukewarm. Sprinkle yeast into water and stir until it dissolves. Add sugar, eggs and salt to milk. Pour into yeast and mix well. Add flour and mix. Store in refrigerator for 24 hours. Divide dough into 4 parts. Roll out dough 1/4" thick on a floured surface and cut into 8 pie-shaped wedges. Start with curved side and roll to a point. Place on baking sheet and brush with melted butter. Let rise at room temperature until double in bulk (1 to 1-1/2 hours). Bake at 450° for 10-12 minutes or until golden brown. Yield: 32 rolls.

Pat is my friend Cheryl's mom, who passed down her cooking skills and this super-simple, super-awesome roll recipe to her daughter.

You can find quicker cinnamon roll recipes than this one from my friend Dave – but few that taste better.

Cinnamon Rolls

David Driscoll, Caledonia

Dough
1 pkg. (.25 oz.) active dry yeast
1 T. sugar
1/4 cup water (warmed to 110° F)
1 pkg. (3.5 oz.) instant vanilla pudding mix, prepare as directed
1/4 cup sugar
1/4 cup butter, melted
1/2 tsp. salt
1 egg, slightly beaten
4-6 cups all-purpose flour

Filling
1 cup brown sugar
2 tsp. cinnamon
1/4 cup butter or margarine, softened
1/2 cup walnuts or pecans, chopped (opt.)

Frosting
1 brick (4 oz.) cream cheese
1-1/2 cups confectioner's sugar
1/4 cup butter, melted
1/2 tsp. vanilla extract
1 tsp. maple extract
1 T. milk

For the dough: In a small bowl, combine yeast, sugar and warm water. Set aside. In a large bowl, mix together prepared pudding, sugar, melted butter, salt and egg. Add yeast mixture and gradually add up to 4 cups of flour to mixture. Mix until smooth, then add enough (up to 2 additional cups) flour to form slightly stiff dough. Turn dough out onto a well-floured surface (or a silicone mat) and knead for 8 minutes or knead in mixer with dough hooks. Place dough into a large greased bowl, cover and allow to rise in a warm place until doubled in size, about 1-1/2 hours. Punch down dough and let rest for 5 minutes. Roll dough out onto a floured surface into a rectangle at least 18" X 16".

For the filling: In a small bowl, mix together brown sugar and cinnamon; set aside. Spread butter over dough; sprinkle cinnamon/sugar mixture and nuts (opt.) evenly over dough. Tightly roll up dough (on 18" edge) and pinch edges together to seal. Cut the roll into 12 equal portions using a serrated knife, dental floss or thread. Place rolls in a greased 13" x 9" pan. Lightly press down each roll. Cover rolls and allow to rise in a warm place for 45 minutes or until doubled in size. Bake rolls in a 350° oven for 20-30 minutes or until golden brown. Check the bottom center to make sure they are not doughy.

For the frosting: In a small bowl, mix frosting ingredients until smooth and spread over slightly cooled rolls.
Yield: 12 rolls.

Banana Nut Bread

Rita Johnson, Ludington

1/2 cup (1 stick) butter or margarine
1 cup sugar
2 eggs
1 tsp. vanilla extract
3-4 large bananas, mashed
2 cups all-purpose flour
1 tsp baking soda
1/4 tsp. salt
1 cup chopped nuts (walnuts or pecans)

Preheat oven to 350°. In a mixing bowl, cream margarine and sugar. Mix in eggs and vanilla. Stir in mashed bananas. Fold in dry ingredients and nuts. Pour into well greased and floured 9" x 5" loaf pan. Bake for 55-60 minutes or until toothpick inserted in center of bread comes out clean. Cool slightly and remove from pan, then cool on wire rack. Yield: 1 loaf or 2 mini loaves.

Poppy Seed Bread

Maxine Wagner, Ludington

1 box yellow cake mix with pudding
1 pkg. (3.4 oz.) coconut instant pudding
1/4 cup poppy seeds
1/2 cup vegetable oil
4 eggs
1 cup boiling hot water

Preheat oven to 350°. In a large bowl, beat cake mix, pudding, poppy seeds, oil and eggs until blended. Blend in hot water. Pour into well greased and floured 9" x 5" loaf pan. Bake for 40-45 minutes or until toothpick inserted in center of bread comes out clean. Cool slightly and remove from pan, then cool on wire rack. Yield: 1 loaf (or 2 mini loaves).

I should never had told Mom they make opium from poppy seed. She stopped baking this for months!

To repeat an earlier theme: anything that has fruits and/or vegetables in it should be considered a health food. That's my story and I'm sticking to it.

Pumpkin Bread

Helen Wilson, Ludington

1/2 cup vegetable oil
1-1/2 cups sugar
2 eggs
1 cup canned pumpkin
1/3 cup water
1-3/4 cups all-purpose flour
1/4 tsp. baking powder
1 tsp. baking soda
1 tsp. salt
1/2 tsp. each ground cinnamon, clove, nutmeg and ginger
1/2 cup raisins

Preheat oven to 350°. In a large bowl, mix oil, sugar, eggs, pumpkin and water. Fold in dry ingredients and mix well. Stir in raisins. Pour into well greased and floured 9" x 5" loaf pan. Bake for 55-60 minutes or until toothpick inserted in center of bread comes out clean. Cool slightly and remove from pan, then cool on wire rack. Yield: 1 loaf (or 2 mini loaves).

Cranberry Nut Bread

Maxine Wagner, Ludington

2 T. butter or margarine
1 cup sugar
1 egg
3/4 cup orange juice
1 T. grated orange peel
2 cups all-purpose flour
1-1/2 tsp. baking powder
1/2 tsp. baking soda
1 tsp. salt
1-1/2 cups fresh cranberries, coarsely chopped
1/2 cup chopped pecans

Preheat oven to 350°. In a large bowl, mix margarine, sugar, egg, orange juice and orange peel. Fold in dry ingredients and mix well. Stir in chopped cranberries and nuts. Pour into well greased and floured 9" x 5" loaf pan. Bake for 55-60 minutes or until toothpick inserted in center of bread comes out clean. Cool slightly and remove from pan, then cool on wire rack. Yield: 1 loaf (or 2 mini loaves).

Cini Minis

Susan Thompson, Scottville

5 T. butter
3/4 cup brown sugar
1/3 cup water
1 cup pecans, coarsely chopped
2 cans (8 oz.) crescent dinner rolls
3 T. butter, softened
1/4 cup sugar
2 tsp. cinnamon

Preheat oven to 375°. In an ungreased 13" x 9" pan, melt 5 T. butter in oven. Stir in brown sugar, water and pecans. Separate each can of crescent dough into 4 rectangles; seal perforations. Spread with softened butter. Combine sugar and cinnamon and sprinkle over the dough. Starting at shorter side, roll up each rectangle. Cut each roll into 4 slices, forming 32 pieces. Place cut-side-down in baking pan. bake for 20-25 minutes or until golden brown. Invert immediately onto a serving plate or jelly roll pan. Yield: 32 small rolls.

Easy Sticky Buns

Deborah Lathrop, Ludington

24 frozen dinner roll dough, thawed and cut in halves
1/2 cup (1 stick) butter, melted
1 pkg. (3.4 oz.) vanilla cook & serve pudding mix
1 cup brown sugar
1 tsp. vanilla extract
1/2 cup pecans, chopped

In a small bowl, combine butter, pudding mix, brown sugar, vanilla and pecans together. Place dough piece halves into the bottom of a greased 13" x 9" baking pan. Pour nut mixture over the dough pieces. Cover and let rise until even with the top of the pan. Bake at 375° for 20-25 minutes. Cool 10 minutes. Turn them over onto waxed paper. Yield: 24 servings.

These ooey-gooey flavor bombs are a 4th of July breakfast tradition on the Wagner homestead patio. Warning: they are addictive!

Mom made loaf after loaf of her apple bread for the "intimate" Christmas dinners she hosted. (She thought 50 or so people was a small gathering.)

Apple Bread

Maxine Wagner, Ludington

1/2 cup (1 stick) butter or margarine
1 cup sugar
2 eggs
1-1/2 T. sour milk*
1 tsp. vanilla extract
1 cup grated unpeeled apple
2 cups all-purpose flour
1 tsp baking soda
1/4 tsp. salt
Multi-colored nonpareils

- Preheat oven to 350°. In a mixing bowl, cream margarine and sugar. Mix in eggs, milk and vanilla. Stir in grated apple. Fold in dry ingredients and mix well. Pour into well greased and floured 9" x 5" loaf pan. Top with multi-colored nonpareils. Bake for 55-60 minutes or until toothpick inserted in center of bread comes out clean. Cool slightly and remove from pan, then cool on wire rack. Yield: 1 loaf (or 2 mini loaves).

- *To make sour milk: combine 1 cup milk with 1 T. vinegar or lemon juice. Let stand 5 minutes.

Think your kids won't eat anything green? Serve them a slice of this pure pistachio pleasure. It was my preferred breakfast bread growing up!

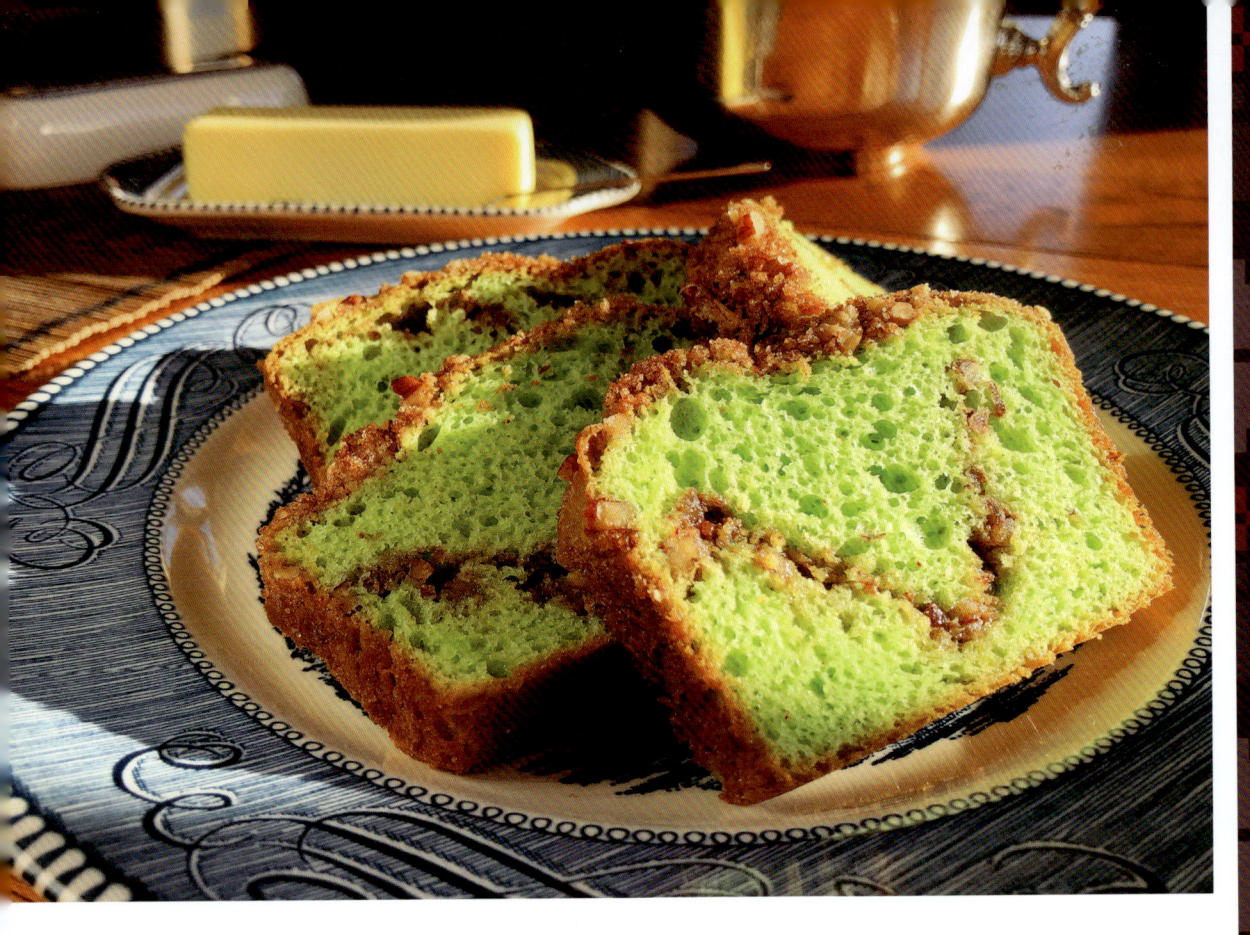

Pistachio Bread

Maxine Wagner, Ludington

1 box yellow cake mix
1 pkg. (3.4 oz.) pistachio pudding
4 eggs
1 cup sour cream
1/4 cup vegetable oil
1/4 cup water
Green food coloring

Streusel
1 cup brown sugar
1 tsp. cinnamon
1/2 cup chopped pecans

- Preheat oven to 350°. In a large bowl, beat cake mix, pudding, eggs, sour cream, oil, water and food coloring until blended. Grease and flour two 9" x 5" loaf pans. Spread half of the batter into the two greased loaf pans. In a small bowl, combine brown sugar, cinnamon and nuts for streusel. Sprinkle half of the mixture over the batter in the two pans saving the rest for the top of the loaves. Repeat the layers, adding the remaining bread batter and the remaining streusel mixture on top. Bake for 50 minutes or until toothpick inserted in center of bread comes out clean. Cool slightly and remove from pan, then cool on wire rack.
- Yield: 2 loaves.

Anybody that grows zucchini needs a go-to bread recipe – my cousin Sue's is the best of the many I've tasted.

Zucchini Bread

Sue Siler, Alto

3 cups all-purpose flour
2 cups sugar
1/4 tsp. baking powder
1 tsp. baking soda
1 tsp. salt
1 tsp. cinnamon
3 eggs, beaten
1 cup vegetable oil
1/3 cup sour cream
3 tsp. vanilla extract
2 cups grated or finely chopped zucchini
1 cup walnuts or pecans, chopped

Preheat oven to 350°. In a large bowl, mix in flour, sugar, baking powder, baking soda, salt and cinnamon. Blend eggs and oil and beat well. Add sour cream and vanilla. Fold in zucchini and nuts. Grease and flour two 9" x 5" loaf pans. Pour batter evenly between two loaf pans. Bake for 45-50 minutes or until toothpick inserted in center of bread comes out clean. Cool slightly and remove from pan, then cool on wire rack. Yield: 2 loaves.

Toffee Coffee Cake

Greg Wagner, Caledonia

1/2 cup (1 stick) butter, softened
2 cups brown sugar
2 cups all-purpose flour
1 egg
1 cup milk
1 tsp. vanilla extract
1 tsp. baking soda
1 tsp. salt
1/2 cup chopped pecans
1 English toffee bar (1.4 oz.), chopped

Preheat oven to 350°. In a mixing bowl, blend butter, sugar and flour; set aside 1/2 cup. To the remaining butter mixture, add, egg, milk, vanilla, baking soda and salt. Mix well. Pour into a greased and floured 13" x 9" baking pan. Combine chopped pecans and candy with the reserved butter mixture; sprinkle over coffee cake. Bake for 30-35 minutes or until a toothpick inserted in the center comes out clean. Cool on a wire rack. Yield: 15 servings.

Orange French Toast

Greg Wagner, Caledonia

1/4 cup butter or margarine
1/3 cup sugar
1/4 tsp. cinnamon
1 tsp. grated orange peel
4 eggs, lightly beaten
2/3 cup orange juice
8 slices French bread

Preheat oven to 325°. Melt butter in a 15" x 10" jelly roll pan. In a small bowl, combine sugar, cinnamon and orange peel, and sprinkle on top of the melted butter. In a separate bowl, mix eggs and juice. Dip bread slices until well soaked. Arrange slices on top of the butter mixture. Bake for 20 minutes. Flip over slices onto serving plate. Yield: 4-6 servings.

Sour Cream Coffee Cake

Greg Wagner, Caledonia

1/2 cup (1 stick) butter or margarine, softened
1 cup sugar
2 eggs
1 cup sour cream
1 tsp. vanilla extract
2 cups all-purpose flour
1 tsp. baking powder
1 tsp. baking soda
1/2 tsp. salt

Topping
1/2 cup chopped pecans
1/4 cup sugar
1 tsp. cinnamon

Preheat oven to 350°. In a large bowl, mix butter/margarine, sugar, eggs, sour cream and vanilla. Fold in dry ingredients and mix well. Spread one half the batter into well greased and floured 9" x 9" pan. In a small bowl, combine nuts, sugar and cinnamon for topping. Sprinkle half of the topping mixture over the batter. Top with the remaining batter. Sprinkle the remaining topping over the batter. Bake for 40 minutes or until toothpick inserted in center of bread comes out clean. Cool slightly and remove from pan, then cool on wire rack. Yield: 9 servings.

I try to eat healthy most of the time. (Really!) But these are two of my favorite indulgences.

This is my globetrotting mother-in-law's nod to her time spent in Michigan. It's a delectable way to enjoy our tart cherries.

Cherry Cheese Ring

Karen Rambo,
Washington Court House, Ohio

1 pkg. (3 oz.) cream cheese, softened
2 T. confectioner's sugar
1/4 tsp. almond extract
1 can (8 oz.) crescent rolls
1 cup cherry pie filling
1 T. milk
1 tsp. sugar

Glaze
1/2 cup confectioner's sugar
1-1/2 tsp. milk
1/4 tsp. almond extract

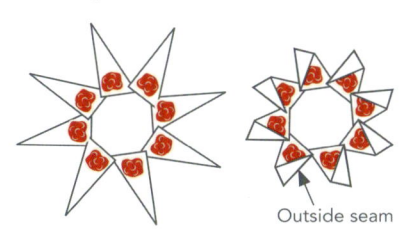

Outside seam

Preheat oven to 375°. In a mixing bowl, beat cream cheese, confectioner's sugar and almond extract until smooth. Separate crescent roll dough into 8 triangles. On well-greased cookie sheet, arrange triangles in a circle with pointed ends (tips) out and opposite ends (bottoms) overlapping slightly, creating a 3" circle in the middle. Spoon cream cheese mixture onto the bottom portion of each triangle. Spoon cherry filling on top of cheese mixture. Fold one triangle over so tip touches the bottom corner. Gently press outside edge and pinch seam. Repeat with remaining triangles. Brush top of crescent rolls with milk and sprinkle with sugar. Bake 15-20 minutes or until golden brown. Let cool. In a small bowl, mix confectioner's sugar, milk and almond extract, and drizzle over the cherry ring. Yield: 8 servings.

Crunchy Granola

Karen Rambo, Washington Courthouse, Ohio

- 1-1/2 cups brown sugar
- 1/2 cup water
- 1 tsp. salt
- 4 tsp. vanilla extract
- 8 cups whole grain oats
- 2-4 cups nuts
  (almonds or pecans)
- Dried fruit (raisins, cranberries, blueberries, tart cherries, etc.)

- Preheat oven to 275°. Line 2 jelly roll pans with parchment paper. In a microwavable bowl, combine sugar and water. Microwave on high for 5 minutes or until sugar is dissolved. Remove from microwave and add salt and vanilla. In a large bowl, combine oats and nuts. Pour sugar mixture over the oats mixture and stir until throughly coated. Spread out onto the pans and bake for 45-60 minutes or until golden brown. Add dried fruit if desired. Store in airtight container after completely cooled. Can also be stored in the freezer. Yield: 18-20 servings.

Baked French Toast

Greg Wagner, Caledonia

- 1/2 cup (1 stick) butter or margarine
- 1/2 cup brown sugar
- 1/2 tsp. cinnamon
- 4 eggs, lightly beaten
- 2/3 cup milk
- 1 tsp. vanilla extract
- 8 slices firm white bread, (such as French bread)

- Preheat oven to 325°. Melt butter in a 15" x 10" jelly roll pan. Combine brown sugar and cinnamon and sprinkle over the butter. In a bowl, mix eggs and milk. Dip bread slices until well soaked. Arrange slices on top on the butter mixture. Bake for 20 minutes. Flip over slices onto serving plate. Yield: 4-6 servings.

Professional opera singer Karen performed around the world and picked up great recipe ideas along the way. This granola gets a Brava!

A great gift idea for co-workers, teachers, etc. — just wrap a few biscotti in a cellophane bag and tie it with a fancy ribbon. Place in a cool coffee cup and voilá!

Orange Cranberry Biscotti

Greg Wagner, Caledonia

2/3 cup sugar
1/2 cup vegetable oil
1 T. grated orange peel
1-1/2 tsp. vanilla extract
2 eggs
2-1/2 cups all-purpose flour
3/4 cup dried cranberries, coarsely chopped
1 tsp. baking powder
1 tsp. baking soda
1/4 tsp. salt
2 cups confectioner's sugar
1/2 tsp. almond extract
1/4 cup orange juice

- Preheat oven to 350°. In a large bowl, stir together sugar, oil, orange peel, vanilla and eggs.
- Stir in remaining ingredients. Place dough on a lightly floured surface and knead until smooth.
- On an ungreased cookie sheet, shape half of the dough at a time into a 10" x 3" rectangle.
- Bake for 25-30 minutes or until a toothpick inserted in the center comes out clean. Cool on cookie sheet for 15 minutes. Cut loaf crosswise into 1/2" slices and place cut sides down on the cookie sheet. Bake 15 minutes longer, turning once, until crisp and light brown. Cool completely. In a small bowl, mix confectioner's sugar, almond extract and juice to make a glaze.
- Drizzle over the cooled cookie.
- Yield: 40 cookies.

Parmesan/Panko-Crusted Cod, page 94

MAIN DISHES

Hawaiian BBQ Ribs

Mitz Lathrop, Ludington

- 2 lbs. country-style ribs (bone-in or boneless according to your preference)
- 3 T. brown sugar
- 2 T. cornstarch
- 1/2 tsp. salt
- 1/4 cup vinegar
- 1/2 cup ketchup
- 1 can (9 oz.) crushed (or chunk) pineapple
- 1 T. soy sauce

- Preheat oven to 350°. In a saucepan, combine brown sugar, cornstarch and salt. Add vinegar, ketchup, pineapple (including juice) and soy sauce. Bring to boil, cook 5 minutes.
- Place ribs into baking pan. Pour sauce over ribs. Cover tightly. Bake at 350° for 2-3 hours. This recipe can be doubled.
- Yield: 2-3 servings.

I don't know if Aunt Mitz ever traveled to Hawaii, but these ribs certainly deliver a taste of the islands. They smell great cooking and they're fall-off-the-bone tender.

I associate Mitz' version of a New England Boiled Dinner with cold winter Saturdays. It would simmer on the stove all day long before we sat down to eat.

Boiled Dinner

Mitz and Gene Lathrop, Ludington

1 smoked ham with bone
6 carrots, peeled and cut into large pieces
6 medium-sized red, white or gold potatoes, peeled and cut in half
6-8 small onions, peeled and left whole
1 head of cabbage, quartered and cored

In large stock pot, place ham and cover with water. Bring to a boil and simmer for 2-3 hours or until the meat starts to fall off the bone. Remove ham from the pot and let it cool enough to handle. Cut the meat into serving size pieces and return to pot along with the carrots, potatoes and onions. Bring stock to a boil, cover, reduce heat and simmer for 45 minutes or until vegetables are tender. Place the cabbage on top of the ham and veggies, cover and let cook for 20 minutes, or until tender. Serve the meat and vegetables with the broth in large soup bowls. Leftover broth, meat and veggies make a great soup.
Yield: 6-10 servings.

Broccoli & Chicken Casserole

Karen Rambo, Washington Court House, Ohio

3 large boneless chicken breasts, cut in 1/2" pieces
2 medium heads of broccoli, cut in pieces and lightly steamed
1 cup mayonnaise
2 tsp. lemon juice
1 tsp. curry powder
1 can (10.5 oz.) cream of mushroom soup
1 can (10.5 oz.) cream of chicken soup
1/2 cup shredded cheddar cheese

Buttered Bread Croutons
3 or 4 slices bread, cubed
2 T. butter, melted
1/8 tsp. garlic salt

Preheat oven to 350°. Cook chicken thoroughly in a pan on the stovetop. Set aside. Steam broccoli and drain. Set aside. In a separate bowl, mix mayonnaise, lemon juice, curry powder and soups. In a greased 13" x 9" baking pan, lay steamed broccoli pieces in the bottom. Lay chicken pieces on top of the broccoli. Spread soup mixture over the chicken layer. Sprinkle with cheese. In a separate bowl, toss bread pieces, butter and garlic salt until coated. Place croutons over the top of the casserole. Bake for 25-35 minutes. Let stand 10 minutes and serve on white rice.
Yield: 8 servings

Almost as easy as frozen pizza but without the maltodextrin, hydrolyzed corn protein, L-cysteine hydrochloride and soy lecithin.

Stir-n-Roll Pizza

Maxine Wagner, Ludington

2 cups all-purpose flour
2 tsp. baking powder
1 tsp. salt
2/3 cup milk
1/4 cup vegetable oil
2 T. vegetable oil
Assorted pizza toppings as desired

- Preheat oven to 425°. In a mixing bowl, combine flour, baking powder, salt, milk and 1/4 cup oil. Stir vigorously until mixture leaves the side of the bowl. Gather dough together and press into a ball. Knead dough in bowl 10 times to make smooth. Divide dough in half. Roll each dough half on a lightly floured surface into a 13" circle. Place dough on pizza pan or baking sheet. Turn up edges 1/2" and pinch. Brush dough with 2 T. oil and place preferred toppings. Bake at 425° for 20-25 minutes. Yield: 2 pizzas.

Easy Slow Cooker Ham

Jeff Wagner, Pentwater

6 lbs. ham, sliced 3/8" thick
3 cans (12 oz.) cola
3 sticks margarine or butter
3 cups brown sugar

- In a slow cooker, layer ham slices. In saucepan, combine cola, butter and brown sugar. Heat until butter is melted and sugar is dissolved. Pour mixture over the ham. Cook on medium to low heat for 2-3 hours. Yield: 10-12 servings.

Need to feed a ton of people ... but you don't want to work too hard? Sloppy Joes to the rescue!

Sloppy Joes

Maxine Wagner, Ludington

1 lb. ground beef or turkey
Salt and pepper to taste
1/4 cup onion, diced
1/4 cup green pepper or celery, diced
1 can (10.5 oz.) tomato soup
2 T. barbecue sauce
1 T. yellow mustard

Brown meat in fry pan with salt and pepper. Add onion and green pepper/celery and cook for about 5 minutes. Stir in soup, barbecue sauce and mustard. Reduce heat and simmer for 30 minutes, stirring occasionally. Serve on hamburger buns.
Yield: 4-6 servings.

Chicken Lasagna

Sue Siler, Alto

6-8 lasagna noodles, cooked
4 chicken breasts, cubed and cooked
1 medium onion, diced
3 T. butter
1 can (10.5 oz.) cream of chicken soup
1/3 cup milk
1 can (8 oz.) sliced mushrooms
1 jar (4 oz.) diced pimentos
2 cups cottage cheese
2 pkgs. (4 cups) cheese - one cheddar and one mozzarella
4 oz. grated parmesan cheese

Preheat oven to 350°. In a large fry pan, sauté onion in the butter. Then add soup, milk, mushrooms and pimento. In a greased 13" x 9" baking pan, place half of the cooked noodles. Then spoon half the chicken mixture over the noodles. Then sprinkle half the cheeses. Then repeat layer. Bake 45-60 minutes. Let rest for 10 minutes. Yield: 4-6 servings.

Almond Chicken

Greg Wagner, Caledonia

1 can (14.5 oz.) chicken broth
2-3 T. cornstarch
1 T. brown sugar
1/4 cup oyster sauce
1 T. soy sauce
1 T. sesame oil
4-6 chicken breasts, boneless, skinned and cut in thin slices
1 medium onion, diced
1 clove garlic, crushed
1/2 tsp. ginger, minced
1 red pepper, thin slices
2 carrots, sliced thin on the bias
1/2 cup celery, sliced thin
1 cup fresh mushrooms, sliced
1/2 cup water chestnuts, sliced
1 (8 oz. bag) sugar snap pea pods
2 green onions, sliced
1/2 cup roasted, sliced or slivered almonds
Steamed white rice

In a small mixing bowl, combine broth, cornstarch, sugar, oyster and soy sauce. Set aside. In large fry pan or wok, sauté chicken in the sesame oil until tender and fully cooked. Remove chicken and set aside. Add a little more sesame oil to the pan. At medium to high heat, add onion and sauté 2 minutes. Add garlic and ginger. Add red pepper and carrots and stir fry for about 2 minutes. Add celery, mushrooms, water chestnuts and pea pods. Sauté for 1 minute. Turn heat to medium and pour broth mixture over the veggies and stir until thickened. Add chicken back in and stir until throughly heated. Serve on white rice. Garnish with green onion and toasted almonds. Yield: 4-6 servings.

This tasty dish is worth all the prep work. The trick is to use high heat at the final stage to sauté it quickly ... then serve right away.

Ever try to stuff cooked pasta shells? Then you'll appreciate this recipe – you stuff the shells first and then cook.

Spinach & Cheese Manicotti

Greg Wagner, Caledonia

- 1 (10 oz.) package frozen spinach, thawed
- 1 jar (32 oz.) marinara sauce
- 1/2 cup red wine
- 1 T. dried sweet basil
- 1 T. sugar
- 1 cup water
- 1 egg
- 1 carton (16 oz.) ricotta cheese
- 2 pkgs. (8 oz.) shredded mozzarella cheese
- 1/2 tsp. salt
- 1/8 tsp. pepper
- 1 pkg. (8 oz.) manicotti shells (14), uncooked

Preheat oven to 350°. Cook spinach according to package directions. Drain well and squeeze dry. Set aside. In medium bowl, mix sauce, wine, basil and sugar. Place 1 cup of sauce mix in bottom of greased 13" x 9" pan. Add water and stir. Set aside. In medium bowl, beat egg. Stir in ricotta cheese, 2 cups of the mozzarella cheese, spinach, salt and pepper, until well blended. Using a table knife, stuff the uncooked shells until full. Arrange in the pan. Cover the shells with the remaining sauce. Cover tightly with foil. Bake for 1-1/4 hours. Sprinkle with remaining mozzarella cheese. Bake 3-5 minutes longer or until cheese melts. Yield: 7 servings.

Quick Stroganoff

Greg Wagner, Caledonia

- 1 pkg. (8 oz.) wide egg noodles, cooked
- 1 lb. ground beef or turkey
- 1 pkg. (8 oz.) fresh mushrooms, sliced
- 6 green onions, sliced
- 1 pkg. brown gravy mix, prepared as directed
- 1 carton (8 oz.) sour cream
- 1/2 tsp. garlic salt
- 1/4 tsp. fresh ground pepper
- 1/4 cup dry sherry
- 1 sliced green onion
- 1 T. chopped Italian parsley

Precook noodles. While noodles cook, brown meat in a large skillet. Add mushrooms and cook 3 minutes. Add onions, prepared gravy, sour cream, garlic salt and pepper. Turn heat to medium. Stir in sherry. Serve over hot noodles. Garnish with sliced green onion and chopped parsley. Yield: 4 servings.

Quick and easy doesn't have to mean dull. (I hate dull.) These dishes are a nice alternative to ordinary comfort foods.

No twirling, less mess — cousin Jeri's casserole lets you (and your kids) enjoy spaghetti without the sauce spatters.

Spaghetti Pie

Jeri Cooper-Claire, Ludington

- 1 pkg. (8 oz.) spaghetti, broken into 2" pieces, cooked
- 2 T. butter, melted
- 1/3 cup grated parmesan cheese
- 1/2 tsp. salt
- 1/4 tsp. pepper
- 1 egg, beaten
- 1-1/2 lb. ground chuck (or turkey)
- 2 T. vegetable oil
- 1 onion, chopped
- 1/4 cup green pepper, chopped
- 1 jar (15 oz.) spaghetti sauce
- 1 tsp. sugar
- 1/2 tsp. oregano
- 1/2 tsp. garlic salt
- 8 oz. cottage cheese
- 4 oz. mozzarella cheese, shredded

Preheat oven to 350°. In a mixing bowl, combine spaghetti, butter, parmesan cheese, salt, pepper and egg. In sauté pan, brown ground meat with oil. Add onion and green pepper and sauté until veggies are tender. Stir in spaghetti sauce, sugar and seasonings. Spread cottage cheese over the spaghetti layer. Top with the meat/sauce mixture. Bake for 30 minutes. Sprinkle with mozzarella cheese and bake for 10 more minutes. Let stand 15 minutes, then serve. Yield: 4-6 servings.

Shepherd's Pie

Jeff Wagner, Pentwater

- 1 lb. ground beef
- 1 medium size onion, chopped
- Salt and pepper to taste
- 1 can (2-1/2 cups) green beans, drained
- 1 can (10.5 oz.) tomato soup
- 5 medium potatoes, cooked and mashed
- 1/2 cup warm milk
- 1 egg beaten
- Salt and pepper to taste

Preheat oven to 350°. In a skillet, brown meat and add onion and seasonings. Add drained green beans and soup. Pour into greased casserole dish. In a separate bowl, mix potatoes, milk, egg, and salt and pepper to taste. Spoon in mounds over mixture of meat, beans and soup. Bake for 45 minutes.

Chicken Fiesta

Greg Wagner, Caledonia

- 1 T. vegetable oil
- 1 lb. boneless, skinless chicken breasts, cut into small pieces
- 1 can (15 oz.) tomato sauce
- 1 cup frozen, whole-kernel corn
- 1 can (4 oz.) chopped green chilies
- 1-1/2 tsp. chili powder
- 1 tsp. onion powder
- 1/4 tsp. salt and pepper
- Tortilla chips
- Garnishes: shredded cheddar cheese, sour cream, guacamole, cilantro

- Heat oil in a large skillet. Add chicken and cook 5 minutes, stirring frequently. Add tomato sauce, corn, chilies, chili powder, onion powder, salt and pepper. Simmer for 10-15 minutes, stirring occasionally. Spoon over tortilla chips and sprinkle with cheddar cheese and other garnishes to taste.
- Yield: 4 servings.

You can serve this as an irresistible party dip or a satisfying dinner. (Don't plan on leftovers.)

This warm and hearty stew dish is a favorite on blustery fall days. Flavor so rich guests will swear it's been simmering all day.

Chicken Cacciatore

Karen Rambo,
Washington Court House, Ohio

1/2 cup flour
1 tsp. salt
1/4 tsp. pepper
2-1/2 to 3 lbs. large boneless chicken thighs or breasts
1/4 cup olive oil
1 can (16 oz.) crushed tomatoes
1 can (8 oz.) tomato sauce
1 cup sliced mushrooms
1/4 cup water
1 can (8 oz.) sliced black olives, drained
1 medium onion, chopped
2 cloves of garlic, crushed
1 tsp. salt
1 tsp. oregano leaves, crushed
1/4 tsp. pepper
1 bay leaf
Fresh Italian parsley, snipped
Hot, cooked spaghetti

Combine flour, salt, and pepper in large plastic bag. Place chicken pieces in bag and toss so meat is coated with flour. In large frying pan, add oil and chicken pieces and brown on both sides. Remove chicken from pan and set aside. In the same fry pan, mix tomatoes, tomato sauce, mushrooms, water, olives, onion, garlic, salt, oregano, pepper and bay leaf. Add chicken pieces back in the sauce and bring to boil. Cover and simmer for 30-45 minutes. Serve over hot spaghetti and garnish with snipped parsley and grated parmesan cheese. Yield: 6 servings.

Parmesan/Panko-Crusted Cod   *Greg Wagner, Caledonia*

4 cod fillets, patted dry
Salt and pepper to taste
1/2 cup all-purpose flour
1/2 cup milk
1/3 cup panko bread crumbs
1/4 cup grated parmesan cheese
1/2 tsp. garlic salt

Tomato Citrus Salsa
1 medium tomato, seeded and small dices
1 orange, cut in small pieces
1/4 cup red onion, diced
1/4 cup red pepper, diced
1 T. cilantro, chopped
1 T. Italian parsley, chopped
1 T. red wine vinegar
1 T. sugar
1/2 tsp. cumin
Fresh lime juice to taste
Salt and ground pepper to taste

Preheat oven to 400°. Lightly salt and pepper cod fillets. In three flat bowls, place flour in first bowl. Pour milk in second bowl. In third bowl, mix bread crumbs, cheese and garlic salt. Dredge each fillet in the flour, completely coating. Run the floured fillet through the milk, then roll and pat through the crumb mixture until fully coated. Place each fillet on a greased, foil-covered pan. Bake for 15-20 minutes or until golden brown. Yield: 4 servings.

For the salsa: Toss all ingredients in a small bowl and serve over fillet.

I used cod here but this breading and salsa would be equally delicious with a Great Lakes game fish.

This was one of my favorite meals as a kid – meaty and cheesy and tangy and hearty. Also: bacon. 'Nuff said.

Mazzetti

Maxine Wagner, Ludington

1 pkg. (16 oz.) egg noodles, cooked as directed
1/4 lb. bacon, diced
2 lbs. ground beef or turkey
1 onion, diced
3-4 stalks of celery, diced
2 cans (10.5 oz.) tomato soup
2 cans (28 oz.) diced tomatoes
1 can (4 oz.) mushroom stems and pieces with juice
1/4 cup red wine
2 tsp. dried sweet basil
Salt and pepper to taste
Grated parmesan cheese

In a large skillet, cook bacon pieces until crisp. Spoon bacon pieces out and set aside. Brown meat in bacon drippings. Add onion and celery; cook until tender. Stir in cooked bacon, soup, tomatoes, mushrooms, wine, basil, salt and pepper; cook for 15 minutes. Fold noodles into soup/meat mixture until noodles are coated. Place in greased baking dish. Top with a good amount of parmesan cheese. Bake at 375° for 35-45 minutes or until bubbly and browned. Yield: 6-8 servings.

Swiss Chard Quiche

Mary Cooper-Nichols, Ludington

1 (9") pastry shell, unbaked
3 cups Swiss chard, stems and leaves, chopped
1/2 cup mayonnaise
1/2 cup milk
2 eggs, beaten
1 T. cornstarch
1-1/2 cups shredded cheddar or Swiss (or combination of both)
1 cup onions, minced
2 cloves garlic, minced
1/2 cup mushrooms, sliced
Seasoned salt and pepper to taste

Preheat oven to 350°. In a large pan, add Swiss chard and about 1/2 cup water and steam until tender. Place cooked chard in a strainer and press out all liquid. In a large bowl, add swiss chard, mayonnaise, milk, eggs and cornstarch together. In a medium pan, sauté onion for a few minutes, add garlic, mushrooms, seasoned salt and pepper. Cook for 2-3 minutes, then drain. Stir the onion/mushroom mixture into the egg/chard mixture. Pour into pastry shell. Bake at 350° for 35-40 minutes. Yield: 6 servings.

Easy Ham Quiche

Mary Cooper-Nichols, Ludington

1 (9") pastry shell, unbaked
1/2 lb. diced ham or pre-browned ground beef
1/2 cup mayonnaise
1/2 cup milk
2 eggs, beaten
1 T. cornstarch
1-1/2 cups shredded cheddar or Swiss (or combination of both)
1/3 cup sliced green onion
1/2 cup sliced mushrooms, sauteed and drained
Seasoned salt and pepper to taste

Preheat oven to 350°. In a large bowl, mix meat, mayonnaise, milk, eggs and cornstarch together. Stir in cheese, onion, mushrooms, salt and pepper. Pour into pastry shell. Bake at 350° for 35-40 minutes. Yield: 6 servings.

Cousin Mary is passing down the Wagner cooking tradition to her children. Recipes like these build their skills.

Cheryl isn't my favorite neighbor because she's a great cook. But that doesn't hurt. She & hubby Jim and Kathy & I have spent many evenings sharing good food and good company.

Sweet and Spicy Chicken

Cheryl Blanchard, Caledonia

6 medium onions, sliced
6-8 boneless chicken breasts
1-1/2 cups ketchup
1/2 cup water
1 cup brown sugar
1 tsp. Worcestershire sauce
1/8 tsp. curry powder
6-8 cups white rice, cooked

Preheat oven to 350°. In a 9" x 13" pan, place onions, then lay the chicken on top in a single layer. In small saucepan, mix ketchup, water and brown sugar. Simmer over low heat for about 5 minutes until the sugar is dissolved. Add the Worcestershire sauce and curry powder and simmer 20 minutes. Pour over chicken and onions. Bake uncovered for 90 minutes, turning occasionally until brown. Serve over white rice. Yield: 6 servings.

Shrimp Creole

Cheryl Blanchard, Caledonia

2 T. olive oil
2 bell peppers, chopped
1 large onion, chopped
1/2 cup celery, chopped
1 can (28 oz.) crushed tomatoes
1/4 tsp. crushed red pepper flakes
1 tsp. salt
1 T. all-purpose flour
1 T. sugar
3 cups peeled shrimp, uncooked
4-6 cups white rice, cooked

In a large skillet, add olive oil and sauté peppers, onion and celery until soft. Add tomatoes, red pepper flakes, salt, flour and sugar, and cook for 15 minutes. Add shrimp and simmer 10 minutes. Hot sauce may be added for a little extra spiciness. Serve over white rice. Yield: 4 servings.

Low-Fat Chicken Enchiladas

Michelle Soneral, Scottville

- 1 pkg. (8-10 count) large tortillas
- 1 T. margarine
- 1/2 cup onion, chopped
- 1 clove of garlic, minced
- 1 can (4 oz.) green chilies, drained
- 1 cup nonfat sour cream
- 2 cans (10.5 oz.) fat free cream of chicken soup
- 1-1/2 cups cooked chicken breast, cubed
- 2 cups (8 oz. pkg.) reduced fat shredded cheddar cheese, divided
- 1/2 cup skim milk

Preheat oven to 350°. Warm tortillas and set aside. In a large skillet, melt margarine and cook onions and garlic until tender. Stir in chilies, sour cream and soup. Mix well. Reserve 1-1/2 cups of sauce and set aside. Stir in chicken and 1 cup of cheese to remaining sauce in skillet. Fill tortillas with chicken mixture and roll up. Place seam side down in an ungreased 15" x 9" glass baking dish. In a small bowl, combine reserved sauce and milk. Spoon over the rolled tortillas. Top with remaining 1 cup of cheese. Bake for 30 minutes until bubbly. Yield: 8-10 servings.

This low-fat version of a Mexican favorite comes from my niece Michele, who has inherited Mom Sue's cooking talents.

The answer to how to feed an army of hungry NOW! kids. This goulash takes about 30 minutes to prepare.

Mom's Quick Goulash

Maxine Wagner, Ludington

2 lbs. ground beef or turkey
1 T. Worcestershire sauce
1 onion, diced
1 green or red pepper, diced
3 cans (10.5 oz.) cream of potato soup or other cream soups (ie., celery, chicken, mushroom)
2 cups canned or frozen mixed vegetables
Salt and pepper to taste
1 pkg. (12 oz.) egg noodles, cooked and tossed with butter
Garnish options: chopped parsley, parmesan or cheddar cheese

In a large skillet, brown meat. Drain fat. Add Worcestershire sauce, onion and pepper; and cook until tender. Stir in soup, vegetables, salt and pepper; cook for 15 minutes. Fold noodles into soup mixture until noodles are coated. Yield: 6-8 servings.

Taco Spaghetti

Sue Thompson, Scottville

1 T. olive oil
1 lb. ground beef or turkey
1 pkg. taco seasoning
1 can (10 oz.) mild diced tomatoes and green chilies
1 T. tomato paste
8 oz. spaghetti, uncooked
3 cups water
1/2 cup shredded cheddar cheese
1/2 cup shredded mozzarella cheese
1 roma tomato, diced
2 T. fresh cilantro, chopped

In a skillet, brown meat with olive oil over medium-high heat. Stir in taco seasoning. Drain excess fat. Stir in tomatoes, tomato paste, spaghetti and water. Bring to boil. Cover and reduce heat and simmer until pasta is cooked through (9-11 minutes). Remove from heat and top with cheeses. Cover until melted. Serve immediately. Garnish with roma tomato and cilantro. Yield: 6 servings.

Chicken Florentine

Kathy Wagner, Caledonia

4-6 thin-sliced chicken breasts
1 pkg. (8-10 oz.) fresh spinach
1 pkg. (8 oz.) fresh mushrooms, sliced
1/4 cup olive oil
1/2 cup white wine
1/2 tsp. garlic powder
1/2 tsp. onion powder
1/2 tsp. dried basil
1/2 tsp. salt
Fresh ground pepper
1 cup shredded Italian cheese

Preheat oven to 400°. Place chicken breasts in a greased 13" x 9" glass baking dish. Pile fresh spinach over the chicken. Then spread the sliced mushrooms over the spinach. In a small bowl, whisk together olive oil, wine, garlic and onion powders, basil, salt and pepper. Pour over the the mushroom layer. Loosely tent foil over the dish and place in oven. Bake for about 45 minutes. Uncover and pile cheese over each chicken piece, then broil for a few minutes until browned. Yield: 4 servings.

This simple and very tasty dish will have people thinking you are a gourmet cook. (I won't tell if you won't.)

Pork on the grill? Absolutely! This spice paste gives the meat a fresh, zesty kick that nicely complements the smoky grill flavor.

Grilled Pork Tenderloin

Pete Siler, Alto

1/2 cup olive oil
1 tsp. dried rosemary
1/2 tsp. chipotle chili pepper
1 T. garlic, minced
1 tsp. sea salt
1-1/2 tsp. fresh ground pepper
2 (1 lb.) pork tenderloins, trimmed
1-3/4 cups raspberry-chipotle sauce

Preheat grill to medium heat (300°-350°). In a small bowl, combine oil, rosemary, chipotle, garlic, salt and pepper. Whisk to mix well. Place pork on a baking sheet and rub generously with spice paste. Place pork on grill. Grill covered, turning often for about 25-30 minutes or until thermometer inserted into the center registers 145°. Meanwhile, pour raspberry-chipotle sauce into a small saucepan and cook over medium heat until warm. Remove pork from grill. Cover loosely with foil and let stand 10 minutes. Cut pork into 1/2" slices and serve with warmed sauce. Yield: 6 servings.

Slow Cooker Pot Roast

Jeanine Petersen, Ludington

1 beef (or venison) roast, any size to fit your cooker
1 pkg. ranch dressing mix
1 pkg. brown gravy mix
1 pkg. Italian dressing mix
1/2-1 cups water

Place roast in slow cooker. In a small bowl, combine all dry mixes and sprinkle on top of the roast. Pour water in the bottom of cooker. Cook on low setting 6-7 hours. Option: add onions, carrots and potatoes for a whole meal. Yield: 4-6 servings.

Mom's Chop Suey

Maxine Wagner, Ludington

1/2 lb. lean beef, chunks
1/2 lb. lean pork, chunks
1 T. olive oil
1 onion, chopped
1-2 cups water or broth
1/4 cup soy sauce
2 T. browning sauce
1/2 tsp. garlic powder
1 tsp. salt
1/4 tsp. pepper
3 stalks celery, sliced
1-2 cans (28 oz.) chop suey vegetables, drained
1 can (8 oz.) bamboo shoots, drained
1 can (8 oz.) water chestnuts, drained
1 can (4 oz.) mushrooms, drained
2 T. cornstarch
1/3 cup cold water
1 can (5 oz.) chow mein noodles
Cooked white rice

In a large pan, brown meat with olive oil. Add onions and sauté a few minutes. Add water, soy sauce, browning sauce, garlic powder, salt and pepper. Cover and simmer for at least an hour. Add celery and simmer for a couple minutes. Add chop suey vegetables, bamboo shoots, water chestnuts and mushrooms. In a small bowl, mix cornstarch and cold water. Mix into chop suey mixture and bring to boil until thickened. Serve over steamed white rice. Top with chow mein noodles and a splash of soy sauce. (Chicken pieces can be used instead of the beef and pork.) Yield: 4-6 servings.

Mom's chop suey was the closest we ever got to Chinese food as a kid – it may not be authentically Asian but it sure is good.

Chop Suey Casserole

Sue Siler, Alto

1 lb. ground hamburger, cooked
1 medium onion, chopped
1 cup cooked rice
1 can (28 oz.) chop suey vegetables, drained
1 can (10.5 oz.) cream of chicken soup
1 can (10.5 oz.) cream of mushroom soup
1 can (4 oz.) mushrooms, drained
2 T. soy sauce
1 can (5 oz.) chow mein noodles

Preheat oven to 350°. In a large fry pan, brown beef. Add onion and sauté until tender. Drain fat from pan, then add the rice and other ingredients. Pour into a 15" x 9" baking dish. Bake for 30 minutes, then stir and top with chow mein noodles. Continue baking 30 addtional minutes or until bubbly. Yield: 8 servings.

These meatballs are bursting with flavor. Add sriracha sauce to make it as hot and spicy as you like.

Thai Chicken Meatballs & Pasta
Greg Wagner, Caledonia

- 1 lb. ground chicken
- 1 egg, lightly beaten
- 3/4 cup panko bread crumbs
- 2 T. soy sauce
- 1 T. fresh cilantro, chopped
- 3 cloves garlic, minced
- 1 tsp. fresh ginger, grated
- 1 tsp. sesame oil
- 1 T vegetable oil
- 1 can (14.5 oz.) chicken broth
- 1/3 cup peanut sauce
- 1/2 tsp. sriracha sauce (opt.)
- 1 red pepper, thinly sliced
- 1 cup shredded carrots
- 3 cups napa cabbage, shredded
- 1 pkg. (8 oz.) angel hair pasta, cooked
- 4 green onions, sliced
- 1 T. fresh cilantro, chopped
- 1/2 cup cashews, toasted

In a large bowl, combine chicken, egg, panko, soy sauce, cilantro, garlic, ginger and sesame oil until well mixed. Shape into 1-1/2" balls and fry in a large skillet with oil until thoroughly cooked. Remove meatballs; cover to keep warm. In skillet, add broth, peanut sauce and sririacha sauce (opt.). Stir in pepper and carrots and cook for 1-2 minutes. Add cabbage and pasta. Add meaballs back in and heat for 1-2 minutes. Serve in large soup bowls and garnish with green onions, cilantro and toasted cashews.
Yield: 4 servings.

It wouldn't be a Midwestern farm cookbook without a meatloaf recipe. This one's "frosted" with buttery mashed potatoes. Oh, yeah.

Meatloaf Delight

Mary Cooper-Nichols, Ludington

- 1 lb. ground round beef
- 1 medium onion, finely chopped
- 1 can (4 oz.) mushrooms, finely chopped
- 8 slices caraway rye bread, finely chopped
- 1/4 cup milk
- 2 eggs
- Salt, pepper, seasoning salt to taste
- 1/4 cup ketchup
- 1/4 cup barbecue sauce
- 8 potatoes
- 6 T. butter
- Seasoned salt
- Milk
- Fresh or dried parsley

- To a large mixing bowl, add beef, onion and mushrooms. In a separate bowl, mix bread and milk. Add the bread mixture to the meat bowl. Add eggs and seasonings. Mix thoroughly. In a parchment-lined loaf pan, press meat mixture. Refrigerate 2 hours. Preheat oven to 350°. Invert meatloaf onto a greased or parchment-lined baking dish. Bake for 45 minutes. Then add a glaze of ketchup and barbecue sauce to the top and sides of the meatloaf. Bake for about another 20 minutes.
- While meatloaf is baking, peel and boil potatoes until tender. Drain and mash. Add butter, seasoned salt and milk (enough milk to make a thick mixture).
- Remove meatloaf from oven, let rest 10 minutes. Then "frost" meatloaf with the potato mixture.
- Lightly sprinkle with additional seasoned salt.
- Return to the oven for about 15 minutes until lightly golden. Sprinkle with parsley, slice and serve.
- Yield: 4 servings.

Cousin Mary manages a lodge not far from Ludington, where she cooks dishes like this for well-heeled members.

Shrimp Pasta Delight

Mary Cooper-Nichols, Ludington

- 1 lb. box linguine, cooked and tossed with olive oil
- 1 lb. frozen shrimp (uncooked, peeled, with tail on)
- 1 T. olive oil
- 2 cups broccoli florets
- 2 cups cauliflower florets
- 2 cups baby carrots, cut lengthwise in 4 pieces
- Salt, pepper, seasoned salt to taste
- 1 T. olive oil
- 1 red pepper, cut in long slices
- 1 yellow pepper, cut in long slices
- 1 medium onion, cut in bite-size slices
- 1 pkg. fresh mushrooms, cleaned and cut in half
- 4 garlic cloves, minced
- 2 cups fresh spinach
- Juice of 1 lemon
- Fresh parmesan cheese

In a wok or large fry pan, add 1 T. olive oil. On medium heat, sauté broccoli, cauliflower and carrots until tender. Lightly season and move to a large bowl. Add 1 T. olive oil and return to medium heat. Add peppers, onions, mushrooms and garlic. Sauté several minutes until desired tenderness. Add to the broccoli mixture and cover to keep warm. Return pan to stove and heat to medium high. Add frozen shrimp. When shrimp turns plump and pink, turn heat to low and add the vegetable mixture back into the pan. Toss in spinach and mix throughly. When spinach starts to wilt, remove from heat. In a large serving bowl, toss pasta and shrimp mixture together. Drizzle with fresh lemon juice and sprinkle with fresh parmesan cheese and serve. Yield: 6-8 servings.

Ricotta Dill Salmon Patties

Susan Thompson, Scottville

- 1 can (15 oz.) salmon, well drained
- 1/2 cup ricotta cheese
- 1/4 cup quick-cooking oats
- 2 egg whites
- 2 T. dried dill weed
- 1 green onion, minced
- 1 T. lemon zest

In a large mixing bowl, add salmon (remove skin and bones if desired). Mash with a fork. Add remaining ingredients and mix well. Form the salmon mixture into 4 patties. Liberally coat a large sauté pan with cooking oil and preheat pan over medium-high heat. Add the salmon patties and cook 5 to 6 minutes per side or until golden brown and cooked through on the inside. Yield: 4 patties.

Crab Cakes & Mango Salsa
Greg Wagner, Caledonia

2/3 cup panko bread crumbs, divided
1 T. Italian parsley, chopped
2 T. green onion, finely chopped
2 T. mayonnaise
1 tsp. lemon juice
1 tsp. Dijon mustard
1/2 tsp. seafood seasoning
1/2 tsp. Worcestershire sauce
1/8 tsp. salt
Dash of cayenne pepper
1 large egg, slightly beaten
8 oz. lump crab
1 T. olive oil

Mango Salsa
1 mango, diced
1/8 cup red onion, diced
1/4 cup red pepper, diced
1 tsp. fresh Italian parsley, chopped
1 tsp. fresh cilantro, chopped
1 T. red wine vinegar
2 tsp. sugar
Salt and pepper to taste

In a large bowl, combine 1/3 cup panko and the next 10 ingredients in a large bowl, stirring well. Add crab and gently stir. Try not to break the lumps of crab. Shape into 4 equal balls. Place remaining panko in a shallow dish and coat the 4 cakes. Gently flatten the balls into 4" patties. In a skillet, add oil and brown patties about 3 minutes on each side. Garnish with mango salsa. Yield: 4 servings.

For the mango salsa: In a small bowl, combine all ingredients.

Fancy, schmancy. But seriously, one of the best crab cakes you will ever eat. The trick: Do NOT over-mix them. You want chunks, not mush.

Cornish miners brought this recipe from the Old World to Michigan's Upper Peninsula. My very good friend Bob's Dad loved pasties (with ketchup!).

U.P. Cornish Pasties

Betty Eames, Door County, Wisconsin

Crust
3 cups all-purpose flour
1 tsp. salt
1/4 cup shortening
1 cup (1 stick) of shortening, frozen until firm (about 30 minutes) and chopped (or grated)
1/2 cup water

Filling
1 lb. lean beef
1/2 lb. lean pork
4 medium potatoes, chopped fine
1/2 rutabaga, chopped fine
1 medium onion, chopped fine
Salt and pepper to taste
Butter

In a mixing bowl, combine flour and salt, cut in shortening, then cut in frozen shortening. Add water gradually. Divide dough into four portions and roll to size of dinner plates. Set aside. Cut meat into small cubes (1/4"-1/2"). Divide potatoes, rutabagas, onions and meat into four portions and build up the filling on the lower halves of the dough. Place half of the potatoes and rutabagas on each pastry and season with salt and pepper. Place a layer of meat on each pastry. Add a thin layer of onion, and season with salt and pepper. Add remaining potatoes, rutabagas, onion and season with salt and pepper. Place two lumps of butter on top of each. Fold the pastry over, moisten the edges with water and crimp to seal. Gash the top of each pasty to vent. Place on cookie sheet with parchment and bake at 400° for about an hour. Yield: 4 servings.

Chicken Lettuce Wraps

Susan Thompson, Scottville

2 T. peanut oil
1 lb. ground chicken
8 green onions, minced
2 tsp. cornstarch
2/3 cup water chestnuts, chopped
3 T. soy sauce
1 T. grated fresh ginger
1 T. oyster sauce
1 large head lettuce leaves
Plum sauce

Warm oil in a skillet over medium-high heat. Add chicken, green onion and cornstarch and cook until chicken is cooked and broken in pieces. Add the water chestnuts, soy sauce, ginger and oyster sauce, and cook for 1 or 2 minutes. Remove from heat. To serve, take 1 lettuce leaf at a time and spoon a heaping spoonful of the chicken mixture into the center. Wrap the lettuce around the filling. May be served with plum sauce. Yield: 6 servings.

Fresh, light and easy to prepare, these wraps are perfect summertime fare – made even better with just-picked lettuce from the garden.

Mom looked down her nose at casseroles – "they're not real food" – but she'd make this one when cleaning out the pantry. It's versatile because you can throw just about anything in it.

Versatile Casserole

Maxine Wagner, Ludington

2 cups diced cooked chicken, turkey, shrimp or crab of your choice
4 boiled eggs, diced
2 cans (10.5 oz.) cream of mushroom soup
2 cups milk
1 pkg. (7 oz.) uncooked macaroni
1 can (8 oz.) sliced water chestnuts
1 pkg. (8 oz.) grated cheddar cheese
1/4 cup green pepper, diced
1/2 cup onion, diced
1/2 tsp. salt
1/4 tsp. pepper

Preheat oven to 350°. In a large bowl, mix all ingredients together and refrigerate overnight. Pour into a greased 13" x 9" baking dish. Bake for 1 hour and 15 minutes. Yield: 8 servings.

Swedish Meatballs

Susan Thompson, Scottville

1/2 cup onion, chopped
1/2 cup almond flour
1 tsp. garlic salt
1/4 tsp. nutmeg
1/2 tsp. allspice
2 T. fresh Italian parsley, chopped
2 eggs
1 T. Worcestershire sauce
1 lb. ground beef
1 lb. ground pork
1 T. olive oil
1 cup chicken or beef stock
1/2 cup sour cream
1/2 cup heavy cream
Salt and pepper to taste

In a skillet, sauté onion in a bit of olive oil and cook until translucent. In a large bowl, combine flour, garlic salt, nutmeg, allspice, parsley (reserve 1 T. for garnish), eggs, Worcestershire sauce and cooked onion. Mix in beef and pork well. Form into 1" meatballs and sauté in large frying pan with olive oil. Once done, place on a platter lined with paper towels. Discard most of the fat drippings from the skillet. Add chicken or beef stock to deglaze the pan. Then blend in sour cream, heavy cream, salt and pepper. Add the meatballs into the sauce and simmer for 15-20 minutes. Serve over zucchini noodles, spaghetti squash or cauliflower rice. Yield: 4 servings.

Sour Cream Apple Pie, page 140

DESSERTS

112

Mom would make this to welcome me back home to Ludington on weekend visits. A delectable way to top off an amazing home-cooked meal.

Boston Cream Pie

Maxine Wagner, Ludington

Cake
6 T. butter, softened
3/4 cup granulated sugar
2 eggs
1/3 cup milk
1-1/2 tsp. vanilla extract
1 cup all-purpose flour
1-1/2 tsp. baking powder
1/4 tsp. baking soda
1/4 tsp. salt

Cream Filling
2 cups milk
1/4 cup granulated sugar
2 T. cornstarch
1/4 tsp. salt
2 egg yolks
1 tsp. vanilla extract

Chocolate Icing
3 oz. unsweetened baking chocolate
3 T. butter
1 cup confectioner's sugar
3-4 T. milk
3/4 tsp. vanilla extract

For the cake: Preheat oven to 375°. Grease and flour a 9" round cake pan. In a large bowl, mix butter, sugar, eggs, milk and vanilla thoroughly. Blend in flour, baking powder, baking soda and salt. Beat mixture for 2 minutes at high speed, scraping bowl occasionally. Pour batter into pan. Bake 25 minutes or until toothpick inserted in center comes out clean. Cool on rack for 10 minutes. Remove from pan, place on rack and cool completely.

For the filling: In a saucepan, combine milk, sugar, cornstarch, salt and egg yolks. Cook over medium heat until mixture thickens and boils. Boil for 1 minute. Remove from heat and stir in vanilla. Let cool.

For assembly: Cut cake in half horizontally with a sharp bread knife. You can use toothpicks to mark middle points around the side of the cake. Place bottom half on serving plate cut side up. Spread filling evenly over the bottom cake layer. Place top cake layer cut side down over filling.

For the chocolate icing: In a saucepan, melt chocolate and butter. Whisk in confectioner's sugar and add milk and vanilla until the mixture is a smooth, spreadable consistency. Spread icing over top of cake, using a metal spatula or back of a spoon, letting some icing drizzle down side of cake. Refrigerate uncovered until ready to serve.

Yield: 8 to 10 servings.

Oatmeal Cake

Maxine Wagner, Ludington

Cake
1 stick butter or margarine
1 cup quick cooking oats
1-1/4 cups boiling water
1 cup granulated sugar
1 cup brown sugar
2 eggs
1-1/2 cups all-purpose flour
1 tsp. baking soda
1 tsp. cinnamon
1 tsp. salt

Coconut Frosting
6 T. melted butter
2/3 cup brown sugar
1/4 cup milk
1/2 tsp. vanilla extract
1-1/2 cups shredded coconut

Preheat oven to 350°. Place butter, oats and water in a covered bowl. Let stand 15 minutes. Add sugars and eggs and mix together. Add flour, soda, cinnamon and salt. Mix well. Pour cake batter into a greased and floured 13" x 9" cake pan. Bake 35 minutes or until toothpick inserted in center of cake comes out clean.

For the coconut frosting: In a small bowl, mix melted butter, brown sugar, milk, vanilla and coconut together. Spread over warm cake. Broil on high until the frosting is browned and bubbly. Yield: 20 servings.

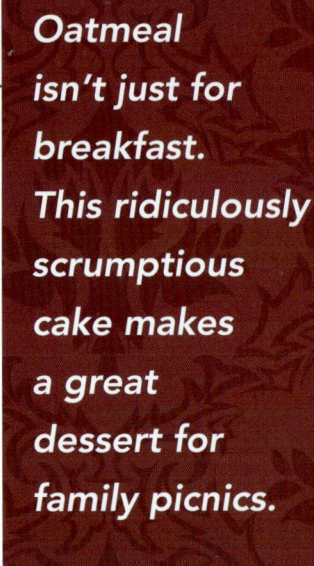

Oatmeal isn't just for breakfast. This ridiculously scrumptious cake makes a great dessert for family picnics.

This sheet cake made an appearance at more Wagner family birthday parties, graduation galas and wedding receptions than I can count. It's still a fave.

Chocolate Sheet Cake
Maxine Wagner, Ludington

1 cup (2 sticks) margarine or butter
1 cup water
4 T. cocoa
1/2 cup sour cream
2 eggs
1 tsp. vanilla extract
2 cups sugar
2 cups all-purpose flour
1 tsp. baking soda
1/2 tsp. salt

- Preheat oven to 350°. In a saucepan, bring margarine or butter, water and cocoa to a boil. Remove from heat and cool slightly. In a large bowl, mix sour cream, eggs and vanilla. Blend in sugar, flour, baking soda and salt. Add cocoa mixture. Mix well. Pour batter in a greased and floured 12" x 18" sheet cake pan. Bake for 20 minutes or until toothpick inserted in center of cake comes out clean. Top with Chocolate Frosting (below). Yield: 24 servings.

Chocolate Sheet Cake Frosting

1/2 cup (1 stick) margarine or butter
4 T. cocoa
6 T. milk
3-1/2 cups confectioner's sugar
1 tsp. vanilla extract
1 cup chopped nuts (pecans or walnuts)

- While sheet cake is in oven, in a saucepan, bring margarine or butter, cocoa and milk to a boil. Remove from heat and add confectioner's sugar, vanilla and nuts. Stir until silky. Pour over warm cake.

Pumpkin Pie Cake
Judy Wagner, Ludington

2-1/2 cups canned pumpkin
4 eggs
1 cup evaporated milk
1-1/2 cups sugar
2 tsp. cinnamon
1 tsp. ginger
1/2 tsp. clove
1 tsp. salt
1 pkg. yellow cake mix
1-1/2 sticks butter, melted

- Preheat oven to 425°. In a mixing bowl, place the first 8 ingredients. Mix well. Pour batter in a greased 13" x 9" cake pan. Sprinkle dry yellow cake mix over the pumpkin mixture. Drizzle melted butter over the dry cake mix. Bake for 15 minutes at 425°. Then turn oven down to 350° and bake an additional 45-50 minutes or until knife inserted into center comes out clean. Yield: 15 servings.

115

Peanut Butter-Toffee-Chocolate

Mocha-Chocolate

Chocolate S'more

Orange Liqueur-Vanilla

Raspberry-Lemon

Chocolate Cupcakes

Meagan Draper, Greenville

1-1/2 cups all-purpose flour
1/2 tsp. baking soda
1/2 tsp. salt
3/4 cup milk
1/2 cup cocoa
1 cup sugar
3/4 cup vegetable oil
1 egg
1 tsp. vanilla extract

- Preheat oven to 350°. In a small bowl, whisk flour, baking soda and salt. In a small pan, heat milk until hot but not boiling. In a large bowl, add cocoa and pour hot milk over it. Whisk until smooth. Let cool slightly. Whisk in sugar, vegetable oil, egg and vanilla. Then whisk in flour mixture until smooth. Divide dough among a 12 paper-lined muffin pan. Bake 18-20 minutes until the tops spring back. Let cool 5 minutes, then transfer to a cooling rack. Yield: 12 cupcakes.

All hail Meagan, Queen of Cupcakes! These are almost as fun to decorate as they are to eat – make it into a family project.

Vanilla Cupcakes

Meagan Draper, Greenville

1-1/2 cups all-purpose flour
1 tsp. baking soda
1/2 tsp. salt
1/2 cup (1 stick) butter, softened
1 cup sugar
2 eggs
2 tsp. vanilla extract
1/2 cup milk

- Preheat oven to 350°. In a small bowl, whisk flour, baking soda and salt. In a mixing bowl, cream butter, add sugar and mix until smooth (about 4 minutes). Beat in the eggs, one at a time. Then add vanilla. Beat in the flour mixture in 3 batches on low speed, alternating with the milk. Beat on medium-high until blended. Divide batter among a 12 paper-lined muffin pan. Bake 18-20 minutes until the tops spring back. Let cool 5 minutes, then transfer to a cooling rack. Yield: 12 cupcakes.
- **Lemon cupcake variation:** Replace vanilla extract with 1-1/2 tsp. lemon extract.

Buttercream Base Frosting

Meagan Draper, Greenville

1-1/2 cups (3 sticks) butter, softened
4 cups confectioner's sugar
3-4 T. milk depending on desired consistency

Note: With frostings where liquid is added, use less milk or omit it if needed.

In a large mixing bowl, combine butter and sugar with a mixer on low speed. Add milk and beat until fluffy. Divide frosting in 5 bowls to create the frosting options to the right. **Depending on the liquid added, add more sugar if needed for desired consistency.**

- **Raspberry frosting for Lemon Cupcake:** Blend in 6-8 large fresh raspberries. Decorate and garnish with a fresh raspberry and a mint sprig.
- **Orange Liqueur frosting for Vanilla Cupcake:** Blend in 2 T. orange liqueur. Decorate and garnish with a thin orange slice and zest, and mint sprig.
- **Mocha frosting for Chocolate Cupcake:** Blend in 2-3 T. strong coffee and 1 T. cocoa. Decorate and garnish with chocolate shavings.
- **Peanut Butter frosting for Chocolate Cupcake:** Blend in 2 T. peanut butter and a dash of salt. Decorate and garnish with chocolate toffee pieces.
- **Marshmallow S'more frosting for Chocolate Cupcake:** In a small bowl, microwave 1/3 cup mini marshmallows until melted. Blend into buttercream frosting until fluffy. Decorate and garnish with a toasted marshmallow and a drizzle of chocolate.

This citrusy twist on one of my favorite cakes is a great way to get your fruits and vegetables. (This claim has not been evaluated by the FDA).

Orange Carrot Cake

Maxine Wagner, Ludington

- 1-1/4 cups vegetable oil
- 3 eggs
- 2 cups sugar
- 2 tsp. vanilla extract
- 1 can (11 oz.) of mandarin oranges, drained
- 1 T. grated orange peel
- 2 cups shredded carrots
- 1/2 cup raisins
- 1/2 cup chopped walnuts or pecans
- 3 cups all-purpose flour
- 1 cup shredded coconut
- 2-1/2 tsp. baking soda
- 1 tsp. salt
- 1/2 tsp. allspice

Preheat oven to 350°. In a large bowl, combine oil, eggs, sugar and vanilla. Mix in oranges, orange peel, carrots, raisins and nuts. Blend in flour, coconut, baking soda, salt and allspice. Pour batter in a greased 13" x 9" cake pan. Bake for 45-55 minutes or until toothpick inserted in center of cake comes out clean. Let cool before frosting. Yield: 20 servings.

Cream Cheese Frosting

- 1 (8 oz.) pkg. cream cheese, softened
- 2 T. melted butter
- 1 tsp. vanilla extract
- 3-4 cups confectioner's sugar

In a mixing bowl, beat until smooth. Add extra sugar until desired consistency. Spread over cake.

Apple farmers have the best apple dessert recipes, and these two are top-notch. Caution: the aroma as they bake has been known to induce drooling.

Apple Dumplings

Maxine Wagner, Ludington

Syrup
2 cups sugar
2 cups water
1/4 tsp. cinnamon
1/4 tsp. nutmeg
1/4 cup butter

Dough
2 cups all-purpose flour
1 tsp. salt
2 tsp. baking powder
3/4 cup shortening
1/2 cup milk

6 apples, peeled, cored and cut in fourths
Sugar, cinnamon and nutmeg
1-2 T. butter

- Preheat oven to 375°. In a small saucepan, place all syrup ingredients and heat until sugar is dissolved. Set aside. In a large bowl, mix flour, salt and baking powder. Cut-in the shortening with a pastry blender until the mixture looks like coarse crumbs. With a fork, stir the milk into the crumb mixture until moistened. On a floured surface, knead dough lightly. Roll out 1/4" thick; cut six 5" squares. Arrange 3 or 4 apple pieces in the center of each square. Sprinkle generously with sugar, cinnamon and nutmeg. Dot with butter. Fold corners to center and pinch edges, closing the apples inside the dough. Place 1" apart in greased baking pan. Pour syrup over the dumplings. Bake for 35 minutes. Serve warm with cream or ice cream. Yield: 6 servings.

Applesauce Cake

Marjorie Sellner, Ludington

1/2 cup shortening
1-1/2 cups brown sugar
1 egg
1 cup thick applesauce
1 tsp. baking soda
2 cups all-purpose flour
1 tsp. cinnamon
1/2 tsp. cloves
1 tsp. salt

Vanilla Frosting:
1/3 cup butter, softened
3 cups confectioner's sugar
1-1/2 tsp. vanilla extract
2 to 3 T. milk
1/4 cup chopped pecans

- Preheat oven to 300°. In a mixing bowl, beat shortening, sugar, egg, applesauce and baking soda. Blend in flour, cinnamon, cloves and salt. Pour batter into a greased and floured 13" x 9" cake pan. Bake 50-60 minutes or until toothpick inserted in center of cake comes out clean. Yield: 18 servings.

- **For frosting:** In a mixing bowl, combine butter, confectioner's sugar and vanilla. Beat at medium speed, gradually adding milk and scraping bowl often, until frosting is smooth and spreadable. Frost cooled cake. Sprinkle with 1/4 cup pecans.

Pina Colada Rum Cake

Maxine Wagner, Ludington

1 pkg. yellow cake mix
1 pkg. vanilla instant pudding mix
1 can (15 oz.) cream of coconut, divided
1/2 cup + 2 T. dark rum
1/3 cup vegetable oil
4 eggs
1 can (8 oz.) crushed pineapple, well drained

Garnish
1 container (8 oz.) whipped cream
Maraschino cherries
1 cup coconut, toasted

Preheat oven to 350°. In a large mixing bowl, combine cake mix, pudding, 1/2 cup cream of coconut, 1/2 cup rum, oil and eggs. Beat on medium speed for 2 minutes. Stir in pineapple. Pour batter in a greased and floured 13" x 9" cake pan or 2 round cake pans. (This can make two cakes or you can layer them). Bake for 50-55 minutes. Cool slightly. Poke holes in the top of the cake about an inch apart. Combine remaining cream of coconut and rum and pour over the cake. Garnish with whipped cream, cherries and toasted coconut. Chill thoroughly. Store in refrigerator. Yield: 16 servings.

This decadent dessert tastes as good as it looks. Don't feel confident about your cake decorating skills? Have a shot or two of rum and you won't care.

Fresh apples and cinnamon wrapped in a buttery, flaky pastry. A perennial Wagner family favorite.

Mitzi's Apple Slices

Mitz Lathrop, Ludington

Dough
2-1/2 cups all purpose flour
1 T. sugar
1/2 tsp. salt
1/2 pkg. (1-1/4 teaspoon) active dry yeast
1 cup butter or margarine (2 sticks)
1/2 cup milk
2 egg yolks, beaten (save egg whites for top crust)

Filling
6-10 apples, peeled and sliced
1 cup sugar
4 T. all-purpose flour
1 tsp. cinnamon
1-2 T. butter

Glaze
1 cup confectioners sugar
1/2 tsp. vanilla extract
1 T. milk

Preheat oven to 350°. In a mixing bowl, combine flour, sugar, salt and yeast. Cut butter in until crumbly, like a pie crust. Blend in milk and egg yolks. Divide dough into two pieces and roll half the dough to fit a jelly roll pan. In a large bowl, combine apple slices, sugar, flour and cinnamon. Pour apple mixture over dough and dot with butter. Roll remaining dough and fit over the apple filling. Cut slits in the top dough to vent. Brush dough with egg whites. Bake for 45-60 minutes until crust is golden and apples are tender. Let cool. In a small bowl, mix glaze ingredients and drizzle over the crust. Yield: 20-24 servings.

Black Forest Torte

Susan Thompson, Scottville

1 pkg. devil's food cake mix
1 can (12 oz.) cherry pie filling
3 cups whipped topping

Prepare cake mix as directed and pour into 2 greased and floured 9" round cake pans. Bake as directed. Cool. Remove cake from pans and cool on wire rack. Place first cake layer on serving plate. On the first layer, spoon 1/2 cup of whipped topping in a 3" circle in the center. Spoon 1 cup of the whipped topping around the edge of the first layer. Spoon half of the pie filling in a circle between the toppings. Place 2nd cake layer on top. Spoon 1-1/2 cups of the topping around the top edge of 2nd cake layer. Spoon remaining pie filling in the center. Chill and serve. Yield: 10 servings.

Devil's Food Cake

Maxine Wagner, Ludington

1 cup sugar
3/4 cup cocoa
1 egg, beaten
1 cup milk
3/4 cup shortening
1 cup sugar
2 eggs, beaten
2 cups all-purpose flour
1/2 cup milk
1/8 tsp. salt
1 tsp. baking powder
1 tsp. vanilla extract

Date Butter
2 cups chopped dates
1/2 cup brown sugar
1/2 cup water
1 cup chopped walnuts

Fudge Frosting
2 cups sugar
1/2 cups cocoa
1/2 cup milk
4 T. butter
1/2 tsp. vanilla

Preheat oven to 375°. In a mixing bowl, combine sugar and cocoa. Beat in egg and milk. Pour into double boiler and cook until thick and smooth. Cool. In a separate bowl, cream shortening and sugar. Add eggs and beat thoroughly. Blend in flour, milk, salt, baking powder and vanilla extract. Add in cooled cocoa mixture. Beat thoroughly. Pour batter in a greased 13" x 9" cake pan. Bake for 25-30 minutes or until toothpick inserted in center of cake comes out clean. Cool slightly. Spread date butter over the cake. Then pour and spread chocolate frosting. Yield: 20 servings.

For Date Butter: In a saucepan, cook dates, brown sugar and water until dates are soft. Add chopped walnuts. Cool and spread on cake.

For Fudge Frosting: In a saucepan, add sugar, cocoa and milk. Boil two minutes. Add butter and vanilla. Stir until smooth. Pour and spread over date butter layer on cake.

I found this long-lost recipe scribbled out in some notes stuffed into an old cookbook. And I'm so glad I did ... the date butter and fudge frosting is incredible!

123

Chocolate Eclair Cake

Maxine Wagner, Ludington

1 box graham crackers
2 pkgs. (3.5 oz.) french vanilla or vanilla instant pudding mix
3 cups milk
1 container (8 oz.) whipped topping

Chocolate Icing
1 oz. unsweetened baking chocolate
3 T. butter or margarine
2 tsp. light corn syrup
1-1/2 cups confectioner's sugar
3 T. milk

Grease a 13" x 9" cake pan. Layer whole graham crackers across the bottom. In a small mixing bowl, combine pudding with milk and mix for 2 minutes. Fold in whipped topping. Spread half of the mixture over the graham cracker layer. Add another layer of crackers and top with the rest of the pudding mixture. Frost last layer of graham crackers with chocolate icing and place on top of the pudding. Refrigerate. Yield: 18 servings.

For the Chocolate Icing: In a saucepan, melt chocolate, butter and corn syrup. Place in bowl and beat in sugar and 3 T. milk until smooth and creamy.

Pistachio Cake

Maxine Wagner, Ludington

1 pkg. white cake mix
1 pkg. (3.5 oz.) pistachio instant pudding mix
3 eggs
1 cup vegetable oil
1 cup ginger ale or lemon-lime soda
1/2 cup chopped pecans

Icing
2 pkgs. whipped topping mix
1 pkg. (3.5 oz.) pistachio instant pudding mix
1-1/4 cups milk

Preheat oven to 350°. In a mixing bowl, combine cake mix, pudding, eggs, oil and soda. Blend on low speed for 1 minute. Beat on medium speed for 2 minutes. Fold in pecans. Pour batter into a greased and floured 13" x 9" cake pan. Bake 30-40 minutes. Cool completely and frost. Refrigerate. Yield: 20 servings.

For the Icing: In a mixing bowl, beat topping mix, pudding and milk until stiff. Spread over cooled cake.

What's better than donuts? Donut cake! It really does taste like your favorite bakery treat.

Aunt Eileen would often drop by for coffee with Mom, bearing homemade goodies like this. Gossip is best shared over sugar, I guess.

Southern Pecan Rum Cake

Eileen Lemire, Ludington

- 1/2 cup (1 stick) butter or margarine, softened
- 1/2 cup brown sugar
- 1/4 cup honey
- 2 eggs
- 1/4 cup water
- 1/2 cup dark rum
- 2 cups all-purpose flour
- 2-1/2 tsp. baking powder
- 1/4 tsp. salt
- 1 cup pecans, coarsely chopped

Glaze
- 1/2 cup sugar
- 1/4 cup butter, cubed
- 2 tsp. water
- 2 tsp. dark rum
- 1/2 cup chopped pecans, toasted

Preheat oven to 375°. In a large bowl, cream butter, sugar and honey. Beat in eggs, then water and rum. Mix in flour, baking powder and salt. Stir in pecans and pour batter into a greased and floured 9" x 5" loaf pan. Bake 50-60 minutes or until toothpick inserted in center of cake comes out clean. Let cool on wire rack. Yield: 10 servings.

For the glaze: In a small saucepan, combine sugar, butter, water and rum. Bring to a boil. Remove from heat; drizzle over warm cake. Sprinkle with pecans. Cool completely on wire rack.

Lane Cake

Mitz Lathrop, Ludington

4 Cake Layers
1 cup (2 sticks) butter, softened
2 cups sugar
1 tsp. vanilla extract
3-1/4 cups all-purpose flour
3-1/2 tsp. double-acting baking powder
3/4 tsp. salt
1 cup milk
8 egg whites

Frosting
1-1/2 cups pecans, coarsely chopped
1-1/2 cups raisins, coarsely chopped
1-1/2 cups shredded coconut
1-1/2 cups candied cherries, quartered
12 egg yolks
1-3/4 cups sugar
1/2 tsp. salt
3/4 cup butter, softened
1/2 cup bourbon whiskey

For the cake layers: Preheat oven to 375°. In a large bowl, beat butter until fluffy. Gradually add sugar and beat until fluffy. Add vanilla and beat until mixture is as light as whipped cream. Sift flour and lightly spoon into measuring cup and level with spatula. Put the measured flour into the sifter. Add baking powder and salt. Sift this mixture onto a large piece of waxed paper. To the butter mixture, add flour mixture; alternating with the milk in small amounts, beating each time.

In a separate bowl, beat egg whites until soft, glossy points (but not dry). With a large spoon, gently fold egg whites into the cake batter until blended. Divide batter evenly between (4) 9" round cake pans (greased and waxed paper lined bottoms). If you only have 2 pans, let half the batter stand in bowl while baking 2 layers. Bake 15 minutes or until batter shrinks from the sides and springs back when pressed lightly with finger. Cool 5 minutes and turn onto wire racks. Yield: 12-16 servings.

For the frosting: In a large bowl, combine pecans, raisins, coconut and cherries. Set aside. In a double boiler, beat egg yolks. Add sugar, salt and butter. Cook in double boiler, stirring constantly until sugar is dissolved and is slightly thickened. Do not over cook. Mixture should appear translucent. Remove from heat and add bourbon. Beat mixture for 1 minute. Pour mixture over pecans, raisins, coconut and cherries, and blend well.

Cake assembly: Place first layer on serving plate. Spread frosting between each layer. Then spread on the top and sides. Cover with cake cover or loosely with aluminum foil. Yield: 12-16 servings.

Aunt Mitzi's original recipe included instructions to imbibe a bit of the bourbon "to make sure it's good." That's her daughter, Charlotte in the photo, applying the finishing touches to her eye-popping creation.

> "Angel food for my little devils," said Mom. Her cherry nut variation was a special treat.

Angel Food Cake
Mitz Lathrop, Ludington

- 1-1/2 cups egg whites
- 1/2 tsp. salt
- 1-1/2 tsp. cream of tartar
- 1 cup sugar
- 1 tsp. vanilla extract
- 1 cup cake flour
- 1-1/2 cups confectioner's sugar

Preheat oven to 325°. In a mixing bowl, beat egg whites until frothy. Add salt and cream of tartar and beat until soft peaks appear. Add granulated sugar 1 T. at a time. Add vanilla with the last addition of sugar. Sift flour and confectioner's sugar over the batter a little at a time and blend in. Pour into ungreased tube pan. Run a knife through the batter to avoid air bubbles. Bake for 40-45 minutes or until golden brown and the top springs back when lightly touched. Cool with pan inverted for 1 hour. Loosen the edges of the cake with a knife, and remove it from the pan. Yield: 12-16 servings.

Cherry Nut Angel Food Cake
Maxine Wagner, Ludington

- 1-1/2 cups egg whites
- 1-1/2 tsp. cream of tartar
- 1/4 tsp. salt
- 1-1/2 tsp. vanilla extract
- 1 cup cake flour
- 7/8 cup sugar (3/4 cup + 2 T.)
- 1/2 cup chopped maraschino cherries
- 1/2 cup chopped pecans

Preheat oven to 325°. In a mixing bowl, beat egg whites, cream of tartar, salt and vanilla until soft peaks appear. Sift flour and sugar and mix in 3 different additions so egg whites don't flatten. In a separate bowl, mix cherries and pecans. Fold into batter. Pour into ungreased tube pan. Run a knife through the batter to avoid air bubbles. Bake for 40-45 minutes or until golden brown and the top springs back when lightly touched. Cool with pan inverted for 1 hour. Loosen the edges of the cake with a knife, and remove it from the pan. Yield: 12-16 servings.

> Mom made this with her home-canned fruit cocktail, but it works just as well with the store-bought version. The vanilla butter sauce is heaven.

Fruit Cocktail Cake

Maxine Wagner, Ludington

1 cup all-purpose flour
1 cup sugar
1/2 tsp. baking soda
1/2 tsp. salt
1 egg
2-1/2 cups canned fruit cocktail, drained and chopped

Vanilla Butter Sauce
1/4 cup butter
1/4 cup whipping cream
1/2 cup brown sugar
1 tsp. vanilla extract

Preheat oven to 300°. Place all ingredients in a mixing bowl. Mix well. Pour batter in a greased 9" x 9" cake pan. Bake for 60 minutes or until done. Serve with whipped cream or warm Vanilla Butter Sauce. Yield: 9 servings.

For the butter sauce: In a saucepan, combine butter and whipping cream with brown sugar. Bring to boil over medium heat. Reduce heat; simmer 10 minutes or until slightly thickened. Remove from heat; stir in vanilla.

This dessert says summer to me, because we'd pick blueberries at the height of the season. Blueberry pie filling means you can enjoy a taste of warm weather all year 'round.

Blueberry Torte

Maxine Wagner, Ludington

Crust
1-1/2 cups graham cracker crumbs (about 24 squares)
1/4 cup sugar
1/2 cup butter or margarine, melted

Cream Cheese Filling
1 pkg. (8 oz.) cream cheese, softened
1/2 cup sugar
2 eggs
1 tsp. vanilla extract
1/2 tsp. ground cinnamon

Topping
1 can (21 oz.) blueberry pie filling
1 container (8 oz.) whipped topping

For crust: Preheat oven to 350°. In a mixing bowl, combine cracker crumbs, sugar and butter/margarine. Press into a greased 11" x 8" baking dish. Bake for 5 minutes.

For filling: In a mixing bowl, beat the cream cheese and sugar until smooth; add the eggs and vanilla. Pour over crust. Bake at 350° for 15-20 minutes or until set. Sprinkle with cinnamon. Cool on a wire rack.

For topping: Spread first pie filling and then whipped topping over the cheese layer. Sprinkle with additional graham cracker crumbs, if desired. Refrigerate until serving. Yield: 12 servings.

Lemon Pound Cake
Mary Lue Dowell, Kalamazoo

- 1 cup (2 sticks) margarine, softened
- 1/2 cup shortening
- 3 cups sugar
- 5 eggs
- 3 cups all-purpose flour
- 1/2 tsp. baking powder
- 1/2 tsp. salt
- 1 cup milk
- 1 tsp. vanilla extract
- 1 tsp. lemon extract

Glaze
- 3/4 cup confectioner's sugar
- Juice from 1 lemon

Preheat oven to 350°. In a large mixing bowl, cream margarine and shortening. Mix in sugar. Gradually beat in eggs, one at a time. Beat well. Blend in flour, baking powder and salt, alternating with the milk. Add vanilla and lemon extract. Pour into a well-greased tube pan. Bake for 60 minutes or until golden brown or until toothpick inserted in center of cake comes out clean. Remove from oven and let cool for about 10 minutes. Then remove from pan and cool on a rack. Place on a serving plate and drizzle glaze over the cake. Yield: 12-16 servings.

Apricot Brandy Pound Cake
Mary Lue Dowell, Kalamazoo

- 1 cup (2 sticks) butter, softened
- 3 cups sugar
- 6 eggs
- 1 cup sour cream
- 3 cups all-purpose flour
- 1/4 tsp. baking soda
- 1/2 tsp. salt
- 1/2 tsp. rum flavoring
- 1 tsp. orange extract
- 1/4 tsp. almond extract
- 1/2 tsp. lemon extract
- 1 tsp. vanilla extract
- 1/2 cup apricot brandy

Preheat oven to 325°. In a large mixing bowl, cream butter and sugar. Add eggs one at a time, beating thoroughly. Blend in sour cream, flour, baking soda and salt. Add flavorings and brandy. Mix until blended. Pour into one greased bundt pan and one small, greased loaf pan. Bake for 70 minutes minutes or until golden brown or until toothpick inserted in center of cake comes out clean. Remove from oven and let cool for about 10 minutes. Then remove from pan and cool on a rack. Yield: 24 servings.

My friend Dave's aunt Mary Lue is an accomplished home baker, as these two recipes attest.

Crumbled Apple

Emma Wagner, Ludington

6 cups sliced apples, peeled
1 T. all-purpose flour
1-1/4 cups sugar
1 tsp. cinnamon
1/8 tsp. salt
2 T. water

Topping
1/3 cup all-purpose flour
1/2 cup quick-cooking oats
1/2 cup brown sugar
1/3 cup butter

Preheat oven to 350°. In a large bowl, mix apples, flour, sugar, cinnamon, salt and water. Spread in greased 9" x 9" cake pan.

For topping: In a separate bowl, combine flour, oats, brown sugar and butter until mixture forms crumbs. Sprinkle over the apple mixture. Bake 45-50 minutes or until apples are tender. Serve warm or cold with ice cream.
Yield: 9 servings.

Grandma Emma experimented with all sorts of apple varieties grown on our 80-acre farm. My favorite for this recipe is the classic McIntosh apple.

Cherry Chocolate Cake

Mitz Lathrop, Ludington

1 pkg. devil's food cake mix
1 can (21 oz.) cherry pie filling
1 tsp. almond extract
2 eggs, beaten

Chocolate Fudge Frosting
1 cup sugar
5 T. butter or margarine
1/3 cup milk
1 cup (6 oz. pkg.) semi-sweet or milk chocolate chips

- Preheat oven to 350°. Spray a 9" x 13" cake pan or 15" x 10" jelly roll pan with cooking spray.
- In a large bowl, combine cake mix, pie filling, almond extract and eggs. Stir by hand until well mixed. Pour into prepared pan. Bake 9" x 13" for 35-40 minutes, bake 15" x 10" for 30-35 minutes or until toothpick inserted in center comes out clean.

For the frosting: In a small saucepan, combine sugar, butter/margarine and milk. Heat to boiling. Boil 1 minute, stirring constantly. Remove from heat, stir in chocolate chips until smooth. Pour over warm cake. Yield: 20-24 servings.

Cherry filling makes this cake oh-so moist — fudge frosting makes it oh-so indulgent. Sweet tooths rejoice!

This is some good sheet – big, rich, moist cakes that graced many a Wagner birthday and graduation party.

Toasted Butter Pecan Cake
Maxine Wagner, Ludington

- 1-1/3 cups chopped pecans
- 1/4 cup butter
- 1 cup butter, softened
- 2 cups sugar
- 4 eggs
- 1 cup milk
- 2 tsp. vanilla extract
- 3 cups all-purpose flour
- 2 tsp. baking powder
- 1/2 tsp. salt

Chocolate Frosting
- 1/2 cup butter or margarine
- 2/3 cup cocoa
- 3 cups confectioner's sugar
- 1/3 cup milk
- 1 tsp. vanilla extract

Toast pecans mixed with 1/4 cup of butter for 20-25 minutes in oven at 350°. In a large bowl, mix softened butter, sugar, eggs, milk and vanilla. Blend in flour, baking powder and salt. Mix well. Pour batter in a greased and floured 12" x 18" sheet cake pan. Bake at 350° for 20-30 minutes or until toothpick inserted in center of cake comes out clean. Top with Chocolate Frosting. Yield: 24 servings.

For the frosting: In a saucepan, melt butter/margarine. Stir in cocoa. Add sugar, milk and vanilla, beating to spreadable consistency.

Chocolate Pound Cake
Mary Lue Dowell, Kalamazoo

- 1 cup (2 sticks) margarine, softened
- 1/2 cup shortening
- 3 cups sugar
- 5 eggs, separated
- 3 cups all-purpose flour
- 4 T. cocoa
- 1/2 tsp. baking powder
- 1 cup milk
- 1 tsp. vanilla extract

Preheat oven to 325°. In a large mixing bowl, cream margarine, shortening and sugar. Gradually beat in egg yolks, one at a time. Beat well. Sift flour, cocoa and baking powder and add alternately with milk, starting and ending with the flour mixture. Add vanilla. In a separate bowl, beat egg whites until stiff. Fold into the cocoa batter at low speed. Pour into a greased bundt pan. Bake for about 80 minutes or until toothpick inserted in center of cake comes out clean. Remove from oven and let cool for about 10 minutes. Then remove from pan and cool on a rack. Yield: 12-16 servings.

We love Judy. We love her even more when she shows up with her famous turtle cake. Simple and simply divine.

Turtle Cake

Judy Wagner, Ludington

- 1 pkg. German chocolate cake mix
- 1 can (14 oz.) sweetened condensed milk
- 1 jar (17 oz.) butterscotch/caramel ice cream topping
- 1 container (8 oz.) whipped topping
- 3-4 English toffee bars (1.4 oz.), shaved or chopped

- Bake cake as directed. While cake is hot, poke holes with the handle of a wooden spoon about 1" apart across cake. In a small bowl, mix sweetened condensed milk and butterscotch/caramel topping and pour over the hot cake. Let cake cool.
- Spread whipped topping over the top and sprinkle chopped toffee bars over all. Refrigerate until ready to serve. Yield: 15 servings.

My cousin Therese was already a wonderful baker at a very young age. She loved to make this pie.

Custard Pie

Therese Cooper, Ludington

1 (9") pie crust, chilled for 1 hour
3 large eggs
1/2 cup sugar
1/4 tsp. salt
1 tsp. vanilla extract
1/2 tsp. nutmeg
3 cups milk, scalded in microwave

Preheat oven to 450°. In a mixing bowl, beat eggs, sugar, salt, vanilla and nutmeg. Slowly pour the scalded milk a splash at a time into the egg mixture, stirring constantly (to avoid the mixture to scramble). Once thoroughly mixed, add to pie crust shell. Place in 450° oven for 10 minutes. Reduce heat to 325° for an additional 25-30 minutes. Insert knife gently into center to test for doneness. If knife comes out clean, it is done. Sprinkle nutmeg over the custard. Allow to cool several hours. Serve chilled or at room temperature. Serve with fresh berries on the side. Yield: 8 servings.

No-Crust Coconut Custard Pie

Ed Wagner, Ludington

4 eggs
1/4 cup butter
1/2 cup all-purpose flour
1 tsp. vanilla extract
1-3/4 cups sugar
2 cups milk
7 oz. flaked coconut

Preheat oven to 325°. In a blender, combine all ingredients. Pour into greased 10" pie plate and bake for 30 to 40 minutes. Yield: 8 servings.

Peanut Butter Pie

Greg Wagner, Caledonia

1/3 cup smooth peanut butter
1 pkg. (8 oz.) cream cheese, softened
1 cup confectioner's sugar
1 (16 oz.) container whipped topping
1 (9") prepared graham cracker crust
15 miniature chocolate-covered peanut butter cups, unwrapped, chopped

In a mixing bowl, mix peanut butter, cream cheese and confectioner's sugar until smooth. Fold in 1/2 the whipped topping until well blended. spoon mixture into graham cracker crust. Place remaining whipped topping over the peanut butter mixture and garnish with chopped peanut butter pieces. Chill for 2 hours or overnight. Yield: 8 servings.

> A great crust is the foundation of any fruit pie. Then fill it with the best Michigan fruit. (We've got lots of varieties to choose from.)

Peaches and Cream Pie

Karen Rambo, Washington Court House, Ohio

1 (9") pie crust shell, unbaked
4 cups sliced peaches
Dash of salt
1 tsp. lemon juice
1/3 cup butter, softened
1/3 cup all-purpose flour
1 cup sugar
1 egg, beaten
1/4 tsp. vanilla extract

- Preheat oven to 425°. In a mixing bowl, toss peaches with salt and lemon juice. Place peach mixture into pie crust shell. In a small mixing bowl, cream butter, flour, sugar, egg and vanilla. Spread over the peaches. Bake at 425° for 12 minutes, then reduce oven to 325° and bake 40-45 minutes until golden brown and bubbling.
- Yield: 8 servings.

Pie Crust

Karen Rambo, Washington Court House, Ohio

2 cups flour
1 tsp. salt
2/3 cup + 2 T. shortening
1/4 cup ice water

- In a mixing bowl, blend flour and salt. Cut shortening in flour with pastry blender until the mixture looks like coarse crumbs. Use a fork to blend water with flour mixture until moistened. Pat into a ball. Cut dough in half. On a floured surface, roll dough out in an 11"-12" circle. Lay dough in pie dish for your favorite pie recipe. Yield: 2 pie crusts.

Cherry Pie

Greg Wagner, Caledonia

2-4 cups tart cherries, frozen
3 T. small pearl tapioca
1-1/2 cups sugar
1 tsp. almond extract
1/2 tsp. cinnamon

- Preheat oven to 400°. In a mixing bowl, mix frozen cherries, tapioca, sugar, almond extract and cinnamon. Set aside while making the pie crust (page 136). Place cherry mixture into raw pie crust. Cut 1/2" strips of dough from the second pie crust and create lattice. Bake 45-50 minutes until golden brown and bubbly. Yield: 8 servings.

The world's best cherry pie, in my not-so-humble opinion. I incorporate different designs into the lattice top to keep it interesting.

Pecan Pie

Maxine Wagner, Ludington

1 (9") pie crust shell, unbaked
3 eggs
1 cup sugar
1/2 cup light corn syrup
1/4 cup butter or margarine, melted
1/2 tsp. salt
1 cup pecan halves

- Preheat oven to 375°. In a mixing bowl, mix eggs, sugar, corn syrup and butter/margarine together. Add pecans and pour into pie crust shell. Bake for 35-40 minutes. Yield: 8 servings.

Pumpkin Pie

Maxine Wagner, Ludington

1 (9") pie crust shell, unbaked
1-1/2 cups canned pumpkin
2 eggs
1 cup whole milk
1/2 cup sugar
1/2 cup brown sugar
1/2 tsp. salt
1 tsp. cinnamon
1/8 tsp. ginger
1/4 tsp. nutmeg
Dash of clove

- Preheat oven to 375°. In a large mixing bowl, mix all ingredients until smooth. Pour into pie crust shell. Bake for 35-40 minutes or until sharp knife inserted in center comes out clean. Serve with whipped topping. Yield: 8 servings.

These pies have graced many Wagner holiday tables. Sure, you can buy them in stores nowadays ... but there's nothing like homemade.

I found this in my grandma Henrietta's recipes — likely from the Depression-era, when fruit was scarce for non-farmers. It's similar to pecan pie, but not as rich.

Soda Cracker Pie

Henrietta Lemire, Ludington

1 cup sugar
1-1/2 tsp. vanilla extract
1/2 tsp. baking powder
1 cup soda crackers, crushed
1 cup pecans, chopped
3 egg whites

Preheat oven to 325°. Generously grease a 9" round pie dish. In a medium bowl, mix sugar, vanilla, baking powder, crackers and pecans. In a separate bowl, beat egg whites until stiff peaks form. FOLD the dry mixture in gently. Do NOT stir or beat mixture. Pour mixture in prepared pie plate. Bake for 30 minutes. Cool and serve with whipped topping and berries. Yield: 8 servings.

Strawberry Pie

Mary Lou Purucker, Milwaukee, Wisconsin

1 (9") pie crust shell, baked
2 quarts strawberries, washed and hulled
1/2 cup water
1 cup sugar
2-1/2 T. cornstarch
1 container (8 oz.) whipped topping

In a saucepan, crush 2 cups of berries and combine water, sugar and cornstarch. Heat over medium heat until mixture thickens, bubbles and turns translucent. Let cool slightly. Arrange remaining berries in cooled pie shell. Spoon the glaze over the berries. Chill completely before serving. Serve with a dollop of whipped topping. Yield: 8 servings.

Sour Cream Apple Pie

Jane Streeter, Grand Rapids

1 (9") pie crust shell, unbaked
1/2 cup sugar
2 T. all-purpose flour
1/8 tsp. salt
1 cup sour cream
1 egg, beaten
1/2 tsp. vanilla extract
2-4 cups apples, peeled and sliced in small pieces

Topping
1/3 cup brown sugar
1/3 cup all-purpose flour
1-1/2 tsp. cinnamon
4 T. butter, softened

Preheat oven to 425°. In a large mixing bowl, combine sugar, flour and salt. Add sour cream, egg, vanilla and apples. In separate bowl, mix brown sugar, flour, cinnamon and butter. Pour apple mixture into pie crust shell. Spoon topping over the apples. Bake for 15 minutes at 425°, then reduce oven to 350° and bake an additional 30 minutes. Yield: 8 servings.

I have tasted a whole lot of apple pie recipes in my time – and my friend Jane gets the nod for the very best. The sour cream makes the difference.

A delightfully old-fashioned pie perfected by my grandma Henrietta, who passed the handwritten recipe down to my Mom.

Graham Cracker Pie

Henrietta Lemire, Ludington

16 graham crackers, crushed to fine crumbs
1/2 cup sugar
1/4 cup butter, softened
2 cups milk, scalded
1/2 cup sugar
2 T. cornstarch
1/2 tsp. salt
3 egg yolks, beaten
2 T. butter
2 tsp. vanilla extract

Meringue
3 egg whites
6 T. sugar
1/4 cup graham cracker mix

Preheat oven to 400°. In a small bowl, mix graham cracker crumbs, sugar and butter. Reserve 1/4 cup of this mixture for the meringue. Press into a pie dish to form a crust. Bake for 10 minutes. Let cool. In a double boiler, scald milk. In a separate bowl, mix sugar, cornstarch and salt. Add to scalded milk and stir until mixture thickens and is smooth. Continue cooking 10 minutes. Blend small amount of hot milk mixture into the egg yolks and stir. Then pour the egg yolk mixture into the rest of the hot milk mixture, stirring continually. Continue to cook mixture for 2 minutes. Cool. Add butter and vanilla and pour into crust.

For meringue: In a separate bowl, beat egg whites until stiff. Add sugar one tablespoon at a time, beating well after each addition. Spread over custard. Sprinkle crumb mixture over the meringue. Bake at 325° for 20 minutes. Chill before serving. Yield: 8 servings.

Lemon Meringue Pie

Henrietta Lemire, Ludington

1 (9") pie crust shell, baked
6 T. cornstarch
1 cup sugar, divided
2 cups water
3 egg yolks, beaten
2 T. cup butter
2 tsp. grated lemon rind
5 T. lemon juice

Meringue
3 egg whites
6 T. sugar

In a double boiler, combine cornstarch, 1/2 cup sugar and water. Cook over boiling water until mixture thickens, stirring constantly. Cook 10 more minutes, stirring constantly. In a small bowl, combine egg yolks and 1/2 cup sugar. Spoon a little amount of hot mixture into the egg yolks, mix and quickly pour back. Cook 2 minutes, stirring constantly. Remove from heat. Stir in butter, lemon rind and lemon juice. Pour into baked pie crust. Refrigerate.

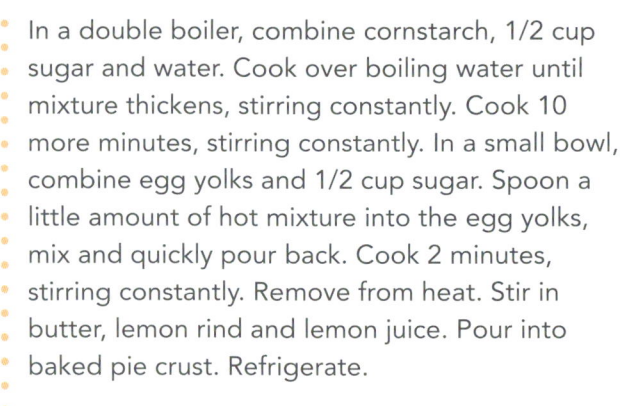

For meringue: In a mixing bowl, beat egg whites until stiff. Add sugar one tablespoon at a time, beating well after each addition. Spread over pie. Bake at 325° for 20 minutes. Chill before serving. Yield: 8 servings.

My mom – the queen of pies – asked her mother to make this pie more than any other growing up. That's a certified Maxine seal of approval!

The reappearance of the "pie plant" was one of the first signs of spring on the farm. I still love rhubarb pies, but these bars are an easier way to enjoy the tart taste of the season.

Rhubarb Dream Bars

Jeanine Petersen, Ludington

Crust
2 cups all-purpose flour
1 cup sugar
1 cup butter, softened

Filling
4 large eggs, beaten
2 cups sugar
1/2 cup all-purpose flour
1/2 tsp. salt
4 cups rhubarb, chopped

Preheat oven to 350°. In a medium-sized bowl, combine flour, sugar and butter until the mixture forms crumbs. Press flour mixture into a buttered 9" x 13" baking pan. Bake for 15 minutes. In a large bowl, mix eggs, sugar, flour and salt until smooth. Fold in the rhubarb. Pour mixture over the baked crust and smooth out with a spatula. Bake 40-45 minutes. Cool. Loosen from sides and cut into squares. May dust with confectioner's sugar. Yield: 15-18 servings.

Helen's Rhubarb Bars

Helen Siler, Merrill

1 cup (2 sticks) margarine, softened
1 cup brown sugar
1-1/2 cups quick-cooking oats
1-1/2 cups all-purpose flour
1/2 tsp. baking soda
1/2 tsp. salt
1/2 cup pecans or walnuts, chopped
2 T. cornstarch
1/4 cup water
3 cups rhubarb, chopped
1/2 cup crushed pineapple, drained
1-1/2 cups sugar
1/2 cup raspberry jam, warmed

Preheat oven to 350°. In a large bowl, cream margarine and brown sugar. Blend in oats, flour, baking soda, salt and nuts. Press 2/3 of the mixture into the bottom of a greased 13" x 9" baking pan. In a saucepan, cook cornstarch, water, rhubarb, pineapple and sugar over medium heat until thickened. Spread the rhubarb mixture over the first oat layer. Drizzle raspberry jam over the rhubarb mixture. Sprinkle the reserved oat mixture over the top. Bake 30-35 minutes. Yield: 15-18 servings.

Cranberry Pie

Michelle Soneral, Scottville

- 2 cups fresh cranberries, chopped
- 1/2 cup walnuts or pecans, chopped
- 1-1/2 cups sugar, divided
- 2 eggs
- 3/4 cup butter, melted
- 1 cup all-purpose flour
- 1 tsp. almond extract

Preheat oven to 350°. Spread cranberries, nuts and 1/2 cup sugar in the bottom of a greased 9" round cake pan. In a separate bowl, mix 1 cup of sugar, eggs, melted butter, flour and almond extract to form a batter. Pour the batter over the cranberries and bake for 40 minutes or until bubbly and golden brown. Yield: 8 servings.

Rhubarb Pie

Sue Siler, Alto

- 2 (9") pastry crusts
- 4 cups fresh rhubarb, chopped
- 1 cup sugar
- 1/3 cup brown sugar
- 1/4 tsp. salt
- 10 T. flour or 5 T. quick-cooking tapioca
- 1/4 tsp. cinnamon
- 2 T. butter

Preheat oven to 400°. In a large bowl, combine rhubarb, sugars, salt, flour/tapioca and cinnamon. Line a 9" pie plate with one of the pie pastries. Pour the rhubarb mixture into the pastry-lined plate and dot with butter. Cut the second pastry into strips and place in a lattice pattern over the top. Bake for 45 minutes or until bubbling and golden brown. Serve with vanilla ice cream while slightly warm. Yield: 8 servings.

Even kids love this sweet-tart pie – we would request it over cake for birthdays. They're mega-popular at local fundraisers.

A Christmas tradition. They just smell like the holidays. Think of them as edible potpourri.

Fruit Spice Bars

Jean Bowles, Grand Rapids

- 1 cup brown sugar
- 1-1/2 cups water
- 1/2 cup shortening
- 2 cups raisins
- 2 tsp. cinnamon
- 1/2 tsp. nutmeg
- 1/2 tsp. ground cloves
- 1/2 tsp. salt
- 1 tsp. baking soda dissolved in 1 tsp. water
- 2 cups all-purpose flour
- 1 tsp. baking powder

Preheat oven to 325°. In a large saucepan, bring brown sugar, water, shortening, raisins, cinnamon, nutmeg and cloves to a boil. Cook for 3 minutes. Remove from heat and let cool. Then add salt and baking soda solution. Blend in flour and baking powder. Pour into a greased 13" x 9" pan. Bake for 35-40 minutes. Cool and frost with a buttercream or cream cheese frosting. Decorate with colored sugars or dried, candied fruit and nuts.

Yield: 32 servings.

Hello Dolly Bars

Helen Siler, Merrill

- 1/2 cup (1 stick) margarine
- 1-1/2 cups graham cracker crumbs
- 1 cup shredded coconut
- 1 cup semi-sweet chocolate chips
- 1 cup walnuts, chopped
- 1 can (14 oz.) sweetened condensed milk

Preheat oven to 325°. In a small saucepan, melt margarine and then add graham cracker crumbs. Stir together until well blended and then pat into the bottom of a 13" x 9" pan to form a crust. Sprinkle coconut over the crust. Then add the chocolate chips and walnuts. Pour the can of milk over the top. Bake for 20-25 minutes or until top is brown. Yield: 24 servings.

Fruit Cobbler

Maxine Wagner, Ludington

2-3 cups fruit, sliced peaches or whole blueberries, raspberries, blackberries or tart cherries
1 cup sugar
1 cup all-purpose flour
1 egg, beaten
1 stick of butter, melted

Preheat oven to 375°. Place fruit in a greased 9" x 9" baking dish or pan. In a small bowl, mix sugar, flour and egg. Sprinkle mixture over the fruit. Drizzle butter evenly over the dry mixture. Bake for 35 minutes or until golden brown. Yield: 9 servings.

Steamed Cranberry Pudding

Betty Eames, Door County, Wisconsin

Pudding
1/4 cup dark molasses
1/2 cup light corn syrup
1-1/3 cups all-purpose flour
2 tsp. baking soda
1/4 tsp. salt
1/3 cup hot water
2 cups fresh cranberries, chopped (or use 1 (16 oz.) can of whole cranberry sauce and add 1/4 cup flour and 1 T. molasses if fresh cranberries are not available)

Sauce
1 cup sugar
1/2 cup cream
1/2 cup butter

In a large bowl, mix together the molasses and corn syrup. In a separate bowl, sift together the flour, baking soda and salt. Add to the molasses mixture. Add the hot water and fold in the cranberries. Pour the mixture into a greased and floured steamed pudding mold or a jello ring mold covered with aluminum foil. On the stovetop, steam for 2 hours in a covered dutch oven or stock pot (low heat) with a couple inches of water on the bottom of the pan. Cool until firm enough to be turned onto a plate.

For the sauce: In a saucepan, warm the ingredients together gently, stirring constantly. Serve warm over the pudding. Yield: 8 servings.

Fresh Michigan fruit makes the best cobblers. (I may be biased.) Fresh-frozen is the next best thing!

Moravian Spice Cookies

Betty Eames, Door County, Wisconsin

1 cup dark molasses
1/3 cup brown sugar
1 tsp. salt
1/4 tsp. ground nutmeg
1/4 tsp. allspice
3/4 tsp. baking soda
3/4 tsp. cinnamon
3/4 tsp. ground ginger
3-3/4 cups all-purpose flour

In a large saucepan, heat molasses to boiling point. Remove from heat. Stir in brown sugar, salt, nutmeg, allspice, baking soda, cinnamon and ginger. Then stir in flour. Work with hands until well blended. Cover and chill overnight. (Dough doesn't hold together until it is thoroughly chilled.) Roll out paper thin in very small amounts. Cut in desired shapes (use small cookie cutters). Place on greased cookie sheets or parchment. Bake 5 or 6 minutes at 375°. May be iced with thin icing or sprinkled with powdered sugar.
Yield: 200 small cookies.

Betty reps the other side of Lake Michigan with these sweets. The super-thin spice cookies originated in the Colonial American communities of the Moravian church.

Grandma Betty's No-Bakes

Betty Eames, Door County, Wisconsin

3-1/2 cups quick-cooking oats
1/2 cup salted peanuts, chopped
1/2 cup smooth peanut butter
2 cups sugar
1/2 cup (1 stick) butter
1/2 cup milk
2 T. cocoa powder

In a mixing bowl, combine oatmeal, peanuts and peanut butter. In a saucepan, heat sugar, butter, milk and cocoa bringing to a low boil for 1 minute while stirring. Pour the boiling mixture over the oatmeal mixture. Stir to combine. Drop teaspoon- or tablespoon-sized balls on wax paper and refrigerate.
Yield: 80 cookies.

Aunt Ve's Brownies

Vera VanDyke, Ludington

1/2 cup (1 stick) margarine, softened
2 cups sugar
1 tsp. vanilla extract
4 eggs
3 T. cocoa
1 cup all-purpose flour
1/2 cup pecans or walnuts, chopped

Preheat oven to 350°. In a mixing bowl, cream margarine and sugar. Add vanilla and eggs and beat. Blend in cocoa and flour. Add nuts. Pour into a 13" x 9" baking pan. Bake for 30-35 minutes.
Yield: 20 brownies.

Candy Cane Cookies
Maxine Wagner, Ludington

1/2 cup (1 stick) butter, softened
1/2 cup shortening
1 cup confectioner's sugar
1 egg
1-1/2 tsp. almond extract
1 tsp. vanilla extract
2-1/2 cups all-purpose flour
1 tsp. salt
Red food coloring

Preheat oven to 375°. In a mixing bowl, mix butter, shortening, sugar, egg and extracts until blended. Add flour and salt and mix well. Divide dough in half. Blend food coloring into one of the halves. Roll 1 tsp. of the red and white dough on a lightly floured surface into strips about 4" long. Twist the two pieces together and roll until it appears striped. Trim ends with a knife for a cleaner look. Place on an ungreased baking sheet and bend dough into a candy cane shape. Bake 9 minutes or until lightly browned. Remove while still warm and sprinkle with granulated sugar. Yield: 3 dozen.

Gingersnaps Cookies
Emma Wagner, Ludington

3/4 cup shortening
1 cup sugar
1/4 cup molasses
1 egg
2 cups all-purpose flour
2 tsp. baking soda
1/2 tsp. cloves
1/2 tsp. ginger
1 tsp. cinnamon
1 tsp. salt
Sugar

Preheat oven to 350°. In a saucepan, melt shortening over low heat. Let cool. In a large bowl, mix shortening, sugar, molasses and egg. Beat well. Add dry ingredients and mix well. Chill dough. Form in 1" balls, roll in sugar and place on greased cookie sheet. Bake 10-12 minutes. They will puff up and crack. Best if they are not over-baked. Yield: 5 dozen.

Soft in the middle, slightly crunchy on the outside ... my idea of the perfect sugar cookie. Decorating them is a family, friend and neighbor affair every holiday.

Classic Sugar Cookies

Maxine Wagner, Ludington

1 cup (2 sticks) margarine, softened
1 cup sugar
1 cup brown sugar
1 cup evaporated milk
2 eggs
5-1/2 cups all-purpose flour
2 tsp. baking soda
1 tsp. baking powder
1 tsp. salt

Icing
4 cups confectioner's sugar
1 tsp. almond extract
1/2 tsp. vanilla extract
Water

In a mixing bowl, cream margarine and sugars. Add milk and eggs and mix well. Mix in dry ingredients. Wrap in plastic wrap and refrigerate overnight. Roll out dough on a floured surface to 1/4" or less thickness. Cut into shapes with desired cookie cutters. Place cookies 1" apart on ungreased cookie sheet. Bake at 425° for 5-7 minutes. Cool on racks. Frost and decorate as desired.

For the icing: In a large bowl, mix confectioner's sugar, almond extract, vanilla extract and enough water to make it thin enough to squirt out of a decorator's tube. Divide among several small bowls and stir in desired food coloring. Use different tubes for different colors. Decorate cookies. Place on waxed paper and let cookies set until frosting is firm. Yield: 8 dozen.

Ohio Sugar Cookies

Emma Wagner, Ludington

1 cup shortening
1 cup sugar
1 cup brown sugar
1 cup sour cream
2 eggs
7 cups all-purpose flour
2 tsp. baking soda
1 tsp. baking powder
1 tsp. salt

In a mixing bowl, cream together shortening and sugars. Add sour cream and eggs, mix well. Mix in remaining ingredients. Chill dough. Roll out dough on a floured surface to 1/4" or less thickness. Cut into shapes with desired cookie cutter. Place cookies on ungreased cookie sheet. Decorate with colored sugar and a raisin in the center. Or decorate with frosting after baking. Bake at 350° for 15 minutes.
Yield: 9 dozen.

> **Grandma Emma lived in Buckeye Country for a time. At least something good came out of her misery.**

Holly Cookies

Sue Siler, Alto

1/2 cup (1 stick) margarine
30 large marshmallows
1/2 tsp. vanilla extract
1-1/2 tsp. green food coloring
4-1/2 cups corn flakes
1 bottle red cinnamon candies

In a large pan, melt margarine and marshmallows. Remove from heat and add vanilla and food coloring. Stir until well blended. Then add corn flakes and stir until flakes are well coated. Form cookie by dropping a teaspoon of dough onto waxed paper into shapes like a holly leaf or a wreath. Place 3 red cinnamon candies on each cookie before the cookie sets up. Let cookies set for 24 hours.
Yield: 18 cookies.

Toffee Cookies

Maxine Wagner, Ludington

3 cups margarine, softened
1-1/2 cups sugar
2 tsp. vanilla extract
3 cups all-purpose flour
1/2 tsp. baking soda
6 chocolate toffee bars, chopped

In a mixing bowl, cream margarine, sugar and vanilla. Add flour and baking soda and mix well. Fold in chopped toffee bars. Divide dough in two. Shape dough into two log rolls. Wrap in plastic wrap and refrigerate overnight. Slice in 1/4" slices. Place on greased cookie sheets. Bake at 325° for 15 minutes.
Yield: 4 dozen.

I already declared my choice for best sugar cookie (page 149). Your palate may disagree – make 'em all and decide for yourself!

White Christmas Sugar Cookies
Mary Jane Millard, Alto

1 cup shortening
2 cups sugar
2 eggs, well beaten
1 tsp. baking soda
1/2 cup evaporated milk
1 tsp. salt
1 tsp. vanilla extract
1 tsp. lemon extract
5 cups all-purpose flour

Preheat oven to 350°. In a mixing bowl, cream together shortening and sugar. Add beaten eggs and mix well. Add baking soda to the evaporated milk and stir. Then add the soda/milk mixture, salt and extracts to the shortening mixture. Mix in flour a cup at a time until dough is not too sticky. Roll out dough onto a floured surface to 1/4" or less thickness. Cut into shapes with desired cookie cutters. Place cookies on a lightly greased cookie sheet. Bake for 7-9 minutes. Yield: 5 dozen.

Holiday Cookie Frosting
Mary Jane Millard, Alto

2/3 cup butter, softened
2-2/3 cups confectioner's sugar
2 to 3 T. milk
3/4 tsp. vanilla extract
Food colorings of your choice

In a mixing bowl, cream butter, sugar, milk and vanilla until smooth. If frosting is too thick, add a little more milk. Divide frosting into several small bowls and color as desired. Frost cookies with different colors.

Raisin Cookies

Kate Murphy, Ludington

1 cup raisins
1 cup shortening
1-1/2 cups sugar
1 egg
1 tsp. vanilla extract
1 tsp. baking soda added to raisin water
3 cups all-purpose flour
1 tsp. salt
1/2 cup chopped nuts

In a saucepan, add raisins, cover with water and bring to boil. Let raisins stand in water overnight. Drain and reserve 1/2 cup of the raisin water for the cookie preparation. In a large bowl, cream together shortening and sugar. Add egg and beat well. Add vanilla and raisin water with baking soda added. Mix in flour and salt. Add nuts and drained raisins and mix gently. Drop by rounded tablespoons on a greased cookie sheet. Bake at 350° for 12-14 minutes. Yield: 3 dozen.

Kate was a cook in the lumber camps in northern Michigan and served these cookies.

Pineapple Cookies

Karen Rambo, Washington Court House, Ohio

1/2 cup (1 stick) margarine, softened
1 cup brown sugar, packed
1/3 cup sugar
2 eggs
1/2 cup evaporated milk
1/2 cup crushed pineapple with juice
1 tsp. vanilla
2-3/4 cups all-purpose flour
1 tsp. baking soda
1/2 tsp. salt

Pineapple Glaze
2 cups confectioner's sugar
1/2 cup crushed pineapple with juice

In a large bowl, mix margarine, sugars and eggs thoroughly. Stir in milk, pineapple and vanilla. Sift together flour, soda and salt, and stir in. Chill for 1 hour. Preheat oven to 375°. Drop by rounded teaspoon onto greased cookie sheets, 2" apart. Bake about 10 minutes or until lightly browned.

For the Pineapple Glaze: In a small bowl, beat confectioner's sugar with pineapple juice until smooth. Frost the warm cookies. Yield: 6 dozen.

Karen's grandparents operated a restaurant during World War I and cooked for 190 soldiers, three times a day. This cookie was beloved by the troops!

Loaded with a variety of textures and flavors, cowboy cookies are big and hearty – just like Texas.

Cowboy Cookies

Sue Siler, Alto

- 1 cup butter or margarine, softened
- 1/2 cup sugar
- 1-1/2 cups brown sugar
- 2 eggs
- 1-1/2 tsp. vanilla extract
- 2 cups all-purpose flour
- 1 tsp. baking powder
- 1/2 tsp. salt
- 2 cups quick-cooking oats
- 1 cup flaked coconut or raisins
- 1 pkg. (12 oz.) semi-sweet chocolate chips

Preheat oven to 350°. In a large bowl, cream together butter and sugars. Add eggs and beat well. Mix in remaining ingredients. Drop in teaspoons onto greased cookie sheet. Bake for 10-12 minutes. Yield: 3 dozen.

Graham Cracker Fudge Cookies

Mitz Lathrop, Ludington

- 2 cups sugar
- 1/3 cup cocoa
- 1/2 cup milk
- 2 T. butter
- 1 tsp vanilla extract
- Graham cracker halves

In a saucepan, combine sugar, cocoa and milk. Bring to a boil and cook for 2 minutes, stirring mixture down from sides of pan. Remove from heat, add butter and vanilla extract. DO NOT STIR! Let cool (bottom of pan is just warm to the touch). Then beat until it begins to lose its gloss. Then quickly spread on graham cracker halves and top with another cracker. If it sets up too quickly, you may add a bit of milk and heat it up again, then let it cool and try again. Yield: 30 cookies.

Oatmeal Crispies

Barb Dawson, Millington

- 1 cup shortening
- 1 cup sugar
- 1 cup brown sugar
- 2 eggs
- 1 tsp. vanilla extract
- 1-1/2 cups all-purpose flour
- 1 tsp. baking soda
- 1 tsp. salt
- 3 cups quick-cooking oats
- 1/2 cup chopped pecans

In a mixing bowl, cream together shortening and sugar. Add eggs and vanilla, mix well. Mix in flour, baking powder and salt. Fold in oats and nuts. Drop by full tablespoons onto lightly greased cookie sheets. Bake on cookie sheet at 350° for 12-15 minutes. Yield: 3 dozen.

No-Bake Fudge Cookies

Mitz Lathrop, Ludington

- 3 cups quick-cooking oats
- 1/2 cup shredded coconut
- 1/2 pecans or walnuts, chopped
- 6 T. cocoa
- 2 cups sugar
- 1/2 cup milk
- 1/2 cup (1 stick) butter or margarine
- 1 tsp. vanilla extract
- 1 tsp. salt

In a large bowl, combine oats, coconut and walnuts. In a large saucepan, combine cocoa and sugar. Stir in milk and butter/margarine. Bring ingredients to a rolling boil. Cook for 2 minutes. Remove from heat and stir in vanilla and salt. Pour over dry ingredients. Stir until coated. Drop by tablespoons onto parchment paper or foil to cool. Yield: 2-3 dozen.

These no-bake cookies are an easy way to satisfy your sweet tooth on a hot summer day.

Lauri's Cowboy Cookies

Lauri Rambo, Caledonia

- 1 cup (2 sticks) butter
- 1 cup brown sugar
- 1 cup sugar
- 2 eggs
- 1 cup creamy peanut butter
- 1 tsp. vanilla extract
- 2 cups all-purpose flour
- 1 tsp. baking soda
- 1 tsp. baking powder
- 2 cups quick-cooking oats
- 2 cups semi-sweet chocolate chips

Preheat oven to 350°. In a large bowl, cream butter, sugars, eggs, peanut butter and vanilla. Mix in flour, baking soda and baking powder. Then add in oats and mix well. Fold in the chocolate chips. Drop onto cookie sheet by large spoonfuls. Bake 8-10 minutes. They are best if slightly underbaked so they are soft and chewy. Yield: 3 dozen.

Two scoops up for these ice cream toppings – a perfect way to top off this cookbook. Thanks for sharing in my family's story!

Hot Fudge

Greg Wagner, Caledonia

1 can (12 oz.) evaporated milk
2 cups sugar
4 oz. unsweetened baking chocolate, broken in pieces
4 T. butter
1 tsp. vanilla extract
Dash of salt

In a saucepan, boil evaporated milk and sugar. Boil for 2-3 minutes. Turn heat to low and add unsweetened chocolate. Stir constantly until chocolate is melted. Remove from heat and continue to stir until mixture starts to appear glossy. This could take up to 5 minutes. Add butter, vanilla and salt. Stir until smooth and glossy. Pour into jars or serve instantly over your favorite ice cream. Stores in refrigerator up to 1 month. Microwave in small glass containers to reheat. Yield: 3 (8 oz.) jars.

Sweet Cherry Topping

Bess Brye, Ludington

3 cups fresh, sweet yellow cherries, chopped
2-1/3 cups sugar
3 tsp. almond extract
2 tsp. red food coloring

In a large saucepan, bring cherries and sugar to a rolling boil. Add almond extract and food coloring. Cook on medium to low heat for 10 minutes, stirring occasionally. Yield: 3-4 (8 oz.) jars.

Index

Accompaniments
Cucumber Relish, 20
Pickled Onions, 18
Shrimp Cocktail Sauce, 17
Sue's Chili Sauce, 21
Sue's Salsa, 19
Tartar Sauce, 17
Zucchini Relish, 21

Appetizers
Beef & Cream Cheese
  Spread, 14
Bread & Butter Pickles, 19
Crab Meat Dip, 12
Dilly Beans, 17
Easy Chili Dip, 13
Fruit Pizza, 22
Gramps Nichols Chip Dip, 15
Jezebel Sauce, 16
Marinated Mushrooms, 14
Party Cheese Ball, 10
Party Meatballs, 10
Sauerkraut Balls, 15
Spinach Balls, 15
Spinach Dip, 12
Vegetable Dip, 11
Zippy Vegetable Dip, 11

Apples
Apple Bread, 75
Apple Dumplings, 119
Applesauce Cake, 119
Crumbled Apple, 131
Mitzi's Apple Slices, 121
Sour Cream Apple Pie, 140

Bananas
Banana Nut Bread, 68

Beans
Baked Beans, 62
Bean & Corn Salad, 45
Cabbage Bean Soup, 54
Calico Beans, 65
Dilly Beans, 17
Three Bean Salad, 40

Beef
Beef & Cream Cheese
  Spread, 14

"Fast Food" Burger Salad, 47
Chop Suey Casserole, 102
Easy Chili, 52
Easy Ham Quiche, 96
Good Ol' Chili, 56
Mazzetti, 95
Meatball Minestrone Soup, 59
Meatloaf Delight, 104
Mom's Chop Suey, 102
Mom's Quick Goulash, 99
Party Meatballs, 10
Quick Stroganoff, 90
Shepherd's Pie, 91
Sloppy Joes, 87
Slow Cooker Pot Roast, 101
Spaghetti Pie, 91
Swedish Meatballs, 109
Taco Spaghetti, 99
U. P. Cornish Pasties, 107

Beverages
Brandy Alexander, 35
Cherry Bounce, 34
Coffee Liqueur, 32
Eggnog, 32
Fruit Punch, 32
Grasshopper, 34
Hot Buttered Rum, 34
Mocha Cream Liqueur, 33
Orange Liqueur, 33
Strawberry Daiquiri, 35
Pete's Tomato Juice, 35

Blueberries
Blueberry Torte, 129
Fruit Cobbler, 146
Fruit Pizza, 22

Breads
Apple Bread, 75
Baked French Toast, 80
Banana Nut Bread, 72
Blue Cheese Rolls, 70
Bread Machine Rolls, 68
Butterflake Dinner Rolls, 69
Cini Minis, 74
Cinnamon Rolls, 71
Cranberry Nut Bread, 73
Crescent Rolls, 70
Easy Sticky Buns, 74
Pistachio Bread, 76
Poppy Seed Bread, 72
Pumpkin Bread, 73

White Bread, 68
Zucchini Bread, 77

Breakfast
Baked French Toast, 80
Cherry Cheese Ring, 79
Cini Minis, 74
Cinnamon Rolls, 71
Crunchy Granola, 80
Easy Ham Quiche, 96
Easy Sticky Buns, 74
Orange-Cranberry Biscotti, 81
Orange French Toast, 78
Pistachio Bread, 76
Sour Cream Coffee Cake, 78
Swiss Chard Quiche, 96
Toffee Coffee Cake, 77

Broccoli
Broccoli & Chicken
  Casserole, 85
Broccoli Cauliflower Soup, 57
Broccoli Salad, 39

Cabbage
Cabbage Bean Soup, 54
Hearty Veggie Soup, 52
Napa Cabbage Salad, 43
Sweet & Sour Cabbage, 63

Cakes
Angel Food Cake, 127
Applesauce Cake, 119
Apricot Brandy Pound
  Cake, 130
Boston Cream Pie, 113
Cherry Chocolate Cake, 132
Cherry Nut Angel Food
  Cake, 127
Chocolate Cupcakes, 116
Chocolate Eclair Cake, 124
Chocolate Pound Cake, 133
Chocolate Sheet Cake, 115
Devil's Food Cake, 122
Fruit Cocktail Cake, 128
Lane Cake, 126
Lemon Cupcakes, 117
Lemon Pound Cake, 130
Oatmeal Cake, 114
Orange Carrot Cake, 118
Pina Colada Cake, 120
Pistachio Cake, 124
Pumpkin Pie Cake, 115
Southern Pecan Rum Cake, 125

Toasted Butter Pecan Cake, 133
Turtle Cake, 134
Vanilla Cupcakes, 117

Candy

9-Minute Fudge, 24
Caramel Delights, 30
Chocolate Covered Cherries, 31
Chocolate-Filled Bon Bons, 30
Double Chocolate Fudge, 24
Graham Cracker Fudge, 23
Mocha Balls, 26
Pete's Peanut Brittle, 28
Peanut Butter Bon Bons, 25
Peanut Candy Squares, 26
Sea Foam, 27
White Chocolate Cherry
   Fudge, 23

Carrots

Boiled Dinner, 85
Hearty Veggie Soup, 52
Orange Carrot Cake, 118

Cheese

Baked Cheese Zucchini, 63
Blueberry Torte, 129
Blue Cheese Rolls, 70
Cheesy Potatoes, 61
Cheesy Spaghetti Squash, 65
Cream Cheese Frosting, 118
Jezebel Sauce, 16
Party Cheese Ball, 10
Parmesan/Panko-Crusted
   Cod, 94
Ricotta Dill Salmon Patties, 105
Spinach & Cheese Manicotti, 89
Wagner Mac 'n Cheese, 64

Cherries

Black Forest Torte, 121
Cherry Bounce, 34
Cherry Cheese Ring, 79
Cherry Chocolate Cake, 132
Cherry Pie, 137
Cherry Nut Angel Food
   Cake, 125
Chocolate Covered
   Cherries, 31
Fruit Cobbler, 146
Sweet Cherry Topping, 155
White Chocolate Cherry
   Fudge, 23

Chicken

Almond Chicken, 88
Asian Chicken Salad, 38
Broccoli & Chicken
   Casserole, 85
Chicken Cacciatore, 93
Chicken Fiesta, 92
Chicken Florentine, 100
Chicken Lasagna, 87
Chicken Lettuce Wraps, 108
Chicken Noodle Soup, 53
Easy White Chicken Chili, 55
Low-Fat Chicken Enchiladas, 98
Mom's Chop Suey, 102
Sweet and Spicy Chicken, 97
Thai Chicken Meatballs &
   Pasta, 103
Versatile Casserole, 109
White Reaper Chicken Chili, 54

Chocolate

9-Minute Fudge, 24
Aunt Ve's Brownies, 147
Black Forest Torte, 121
Boston Cream Pie, 113
Cherry Chocolate Cake, 132
Chocolate Covered
   Cherries, 31
Chocolate Cupcakes, 116
Chocolate Eclair Cake, 124
Chocolate-Filled Bon Bons, 30
Chocolate Pound Cake, 133
Chocolate Sheet Cake, 115
Cowboy Cookies, 153
Devil's Food Cake, 122
Double Chocolate Fudge, 30
Graham Cracker Fudge, 23
Graham Cracker Fudge
   Cookies, 153
Hello Dolly Bars, 145
Lauri's Cowboy Cookies, 154
No-Bake Fudge Cookies, 154

Coconut

Cowboy Cookies, 153
Hello Dolly Bars, 145
Lane Cake, 126
No-Crust Coconut Custard
   Pie, 135
Oatmeal Cake, 114
Pina Colada Cake, 120

Coffee Cakes

Toffee Coffee Cake, 77
Sour Cream Coffee Cake, 78

Cookies

Candy Cane Cookies, 148
Classic Sugar Cookies, 149
Cowboy Cookies, 153
Gingersnaps Cookies, 148
Graham Cracker Fudge
   Cookies, 153
Grandma Betty's No-Bakes, 147
Holiday Cookie Frosting, 151
Holly Cookies, 150
Lauri's Cowboy Cookies, 154
Moravian Spice Cookies, 147
No-Bake Fudge Cookies, 154
Oatmeal Crispies, 154
Ohio Sugar Cookies, 150
Orange-Cranberry Biscotti, 77
Pineapple Cookies, 152
Raisin Cookies, 152
Toffee Cookies, 150
White Christmas Sugar
   Cookies, 151

Cookies, Bar

Aunt Ve's Brownies, 147
Fruit Spice Bars, 145
Helen's Rhubarb Bars, 143
Hello Dolly Bars, 145
Rhubarb Dream Bars, 143

Corn

Bean & Corn Salad, 45
Esquites (Corn) Salad, 44

Cranberries

Cranberry Nut Bread, 73
Cranberry Pie, 144
Orange-Cranberry Biscotti, 81
Steamed Cranberry
   Pudding, 146

Desserts

Apple Dumplings, 119
Aunt Ve's Brownies, 147
Black Forest Torte, 121
Crumbled Apple, 131
Fruit Cobbler, 146
Mitzi's Apple Slices, 121
Steamed Cranberry
   Pudding, 146

157

Fish
Parmesan/Panko-Crusted Cod, 94
Ricotta Dill Salmon Patties, 105

Frostings & Icings
Buttercream Base Frosting, 117
Chocolate Fudge Frosting, 132
Chocolate Frosting, 133
Chocolate Icing, 113, 124
Chocolate Sheet Cake Frosting, 115
Coconut Frosting, 114
Cream Cheese Frosting, 118
Fudge Frosting, 122
Holiday Cookie Frosting, 151
Lane Cake Frosting, 126
Lemon Glaze, 130
Marshmallow S'more Frosting, 117
Mocha Frosting, 117
Orange Liquer Frosting, 117
Peanut Butter Frosting, 117
Pistachio Frosting, 124
Raspberry Frosting, 117
Rum Glaze, 125
Sugar Cookie Icing, 149
Vanilla Butter Sauce, 128
Vanilla Frosting, 119

Fruit
Fruit Cobbler, 146
Fruit Cocktail Cake, 128
Fruit Pizza, 22
Fruit Spice Bars, 145

Gelatins
7-Layer Gelatin, 51
Aunt Ve's Gelatin Salad, 50
Raspberry-Cranberry Gelatin, 51

Lemons
Lemon Cupcakes, 117
Lemon Meringue Pie, 142

Oranges
Orange-Cranberry Biscotti, 81
Orange Carrot Cake, 118
Orange French Toast, 78

Pasta
Chicken Cacciatore, 93
Chicken Lasagna, 87
Greek Spinach Pasta Salad, 46
Macaroni Salad, 41
Mazzetti, 95
Quick Stroganoff, 90
Shrimp Pasta Delight, 105
Spaghetti Pie, 91
Spinach & Cheese Manicotti, 89
Taco Spaghetti, 99
Thai Chicken Meatballs & Pasta, 103
Wagner Mac 'n Cheese, 64

Peaches
Peaches and Cream Pie, 136

Peanut Butter
Grandma Betty's No-Bakes, 147
Lauri's Cowboy Cookies, 154
Peanut Butter Bon Bons, 25
Peanut Butter Pie, 135
Peanut Candy Squares, 26

Pears
Spinach Pear Salad, 41

Pickled Produce
Pickled Beets, 18
Pickled Onions, 18
Bread & Butter Pickles, 19
Cucumber Relish, 20
Dilly Beans, 17

Pies
Cherry Pie, 137
Cranberry Pie, 144
Custard Pie, 135
Graham Cracker Pie, 141
Lemon Meringue Pie, 142
No-Crust Coconut Custard Pie, 135
Peaches and Cream Pie, 136
Peanut Butter Pie, 135
Pecan Pie, 138
Pie Crust, 136
Pumpkin Pie, 138
Rhubarb Pie, 144
Shepherd's Pie, 91
Soda Cracker Pie, 139
Sour Cream Apple Pie, 140
Spaghetti Pie, 91
Strawberry Pie, 139
Tomato Pie, 62

Pineapple
Glorified Rice, 60
Pina Colada Cake, 120
Pineapple Cookies, 152

Pizza
Fruit Pizza, 22
Stir-n-Roll Pizza, 86
Veggie Pizza, 16

Pork
Boiled Dinner, 85
Easy Ham Quiche, 96
Easy Slow Cooker Ham, 86
Grilled Pork Tenderloin, 101
Hawaiian BBQ Ribs, 84
Mom's Chop Suey, 102
U. P. Cornish Pasties, 107

Potatoes
Boiled Dinner, 85
Cheesy Potatoes, 61
Classic Potato Salad, 47
Hot German Potato Salad, 85
Meatloaf Delight, 104
Potato Casserole, 61
Potato-Sauerkraut Soup, 55
Shepherd's Pie, 91
Sweet Potato Soufflé, 64
U. P. Cornish Pasties, 107

Pumpkin
Pumpkin Bread, 73
Pumpkin Pie, 138
Pumpkin Pie Cake, 115

Quiche
Easy Ham Quiche, 96
Swiss Chard Quiche, 96

Raspberries
Fruit Cobbler, 146
Helen's Rhubarb Bars, 143
Raspberry Frosting, 117